CONSUMER GUIDE TO

ASSET
PROTECTION

A STEP-BY-STEP GUIDE TO
PRESERVING
WEALTH

JEFFREY MATSEN

Cover and interior design by Anthony Nuccio/Ankerwycke.

In 1215, the Magna Carta was sealed underneath the ancient Ankerwycke Yew tree, starting the process that led to rule by constitutional law—in effect, giving rights and the law to the people. Today, the ABA's Ankerwycke line of books continues to bring the law to the people. With legal fiction, true crime books, popular legal histories, public policy handbooks, and prescriptive guides to current legal and business issues, Ankerwycke is a contemporary and innovative line of books for everyone from a trusted and vested authority.

Printed in the United States of America.
26 25 24   10 9 8 7

ISBN: 978-1-62722-765-0
e-ISBN: 978-1-62722-766-7

Library of Congress Cataloging-in-Publication Data

Matsen, Jeffrey R., author.
   The American Bar Association consumer guide to asset protection planning : a step-by-step guide to preserving wealth / Jeffrey R. Matsen, JD.
      pages cm
   Includes bibliographical references and index.
   ISBN 978-1-62722-765-0 (alk. paper)
   1. Executions (Law)—United States. 2. Fraudulent conveyances—United States. 3. Debtor and creditor—United States. 4. Self-settled trusts—United States. 5. Estate planning—United States. I. Title.
   KF9025.M38 2015
   346.7305—dc23

                                                                                    2015021654

Discounts are available for books ordered in bulk. Special consideration is given to state bars, CLE programs, and other bar-related organizations. Inquire at Book Publishing, ABA Publishing, American Bar Association, 321 N. Clark Street, Chicago, Illinois 60654-7598.

www.ShopABA.org

Contents

Preface   vii

Chapter 1. Introduction   1

Asset Protection Planning   1
Shield of Liability   1
Inside and Outside Creditors   3
    Inside Creditors   3
    Outside Creditors   4
A Comprehensive Example   4
    1. Scott's Architectural Practice and the Ramifications of Operating as the Sole Proprietor   5
    2. Estate Planning   5
    3. Exemption and Marital Planning   5
    4. Liability-Protected Entities   5
    5. Domestic Asset Protection Trusts   5
    6. Offshore Planning   5
    7. Advanced Estate Planning   6
    8. Just What the Doctor Ordered   6
    9. Putting It All Together   6

Chapter 2. Why Plan? The Need for Asset Protection   7

The Reasons   7
    1. Victim-Oriented Society   7
    2. Plaintiff Lawyers   8
    3. Expanding Theories of Liability   8
    4. Deep-Pocket Theory   8
    5. Increased Notoriety   8
    Who are the Victims of Lawsuit Onslaughts? Who Needs to Protect and Defend their
    Amassed Assets and Properties?   9
Creditors, Discovery and Remedies   9

Chapter 3. The Limitations   13

Fraudulent Transfer Law   13
Bankruptcy   16
Money Laundering and Other Criminal Statutes   17

Chapter 4. The Ladder of Success   **19**

The Multi-Tiered Approach   19
   Step One: The Business Entity   *20*
   Step Two: Basic Estate Planning   *21*
   Step Three: Exemptions and Marital Planning   *21*
   Step Four: Liability-Protected Entities for Investment Assets   *21*
   Step Five: Domestic Modular Planning with Asset Protection Trusts   *21*
   Step Six: Offshore Modular Planning with Offshore Asset Protection Trust   *21*
   Step Seven: Advanced Estate Planning Techniques   *22*
   Physician Planning   *22*
   Putting It All Together   *22*
   The Ladder   *22*

Chapter 5. Step One on the Ladder: The Operating Business Entity   **23**

Sole Proprietorship   24
General Partnership   25
Limited Partnership   25
Limited Liability Company   26
Corporation   26
Limited Liability Partnership   27
Selecting the Proper Business Entity   27

Chapter 6. Step Two on the Ladder: Basic Estate Planning   **29**

Foundational Documents   29
   Will and Powers of Attorney   *30*
   Healthcare Directives or Medical Powers of Attorney   *31*
   The Revocable Living Trust   *31*

Chapter 7. Step Three on the Ladder: Bankruptcy Considerations, Exemptions, and Marital Planning   **35**

Bankruptcy Considerations   35
Other Exemptions and Protections   36
Adequate Insurance   37
Joint Ownership of Property   37
Marital Planning   38

Chapter 8. Step Four on the Ladder: Liability Protective Entities for Investment Assets   **39**

Real Estate Assets   40
Segregating Assets into Multiple Liability-Protected Entities   41
The Charging Order and Protection against Outside Debts   41
What Is a Charging Order?   42
Historical Background of the Charging Order   42
Forum Shopping   44
The Series LLC   44

Uses   45
Conclusion   46
   One Final Word of Caution   46

Chapter 9. Step Five on the Ladder: Domestic Asset Protection Trusts and
Modular Planning Utilizing LLCs   **49**

Setting Up and Maintaining Domestic Asset Protection Trusts   50
   Consequences of Utilizing Domestic Asset Protection Trusts   51
   Modular Structuring Utilizing DAPT and LLCs   52
Divided You Stand; United You Fall   52
   Hypothetical Case Study No. 1   53
   Hypothetical Case Study No. 2   53
   Hypothetical Case Study No. 3   54
The Trust Protector   55

Chapter 10. Step Six on the Ladder: The Offshore Asset Protection Trust and the Modular
Planning that Accompanies It   **57**

Setting Up and Maintaining the Foreign Asset Protection Trust   58
Factors and Jurisdiction-Selection Process   59
Tax Considerations   60
The Cook Islands: The Best Offshore Jurisdiction   60
Issues of Contempt of the Foreign Asset Protection Trusts   61
   The Anderson Case   62
   The Lawrence Case   62
Offshore Modular Planning   63

Chapter 11. Advanced Estate Planning Techniques   **65**

The Irrevocable Life Insurance Trust   65
Family Limited Partnerships and LLCs   66
Charitable Remainder Trusts and Charitable Lead Trusts   67
Grantor Retained Annuity Trust   67
Qualified Personal Residence Trust   68
The Intentionally Defective Irrevocable Trust   68

Chapter 12. Just What The Doctor Ordered: Some Special Issues and Strategies
for Physicians and Dentists   **71**

The Medical Practice   72
   1. Independent Contractor   72
   2. Equipment   73
   3. Professional Relationship Agreements   73
   4. Surgical Center   73
Malpractice   74
   Why Should Doctors Worry?   74
Non-Practice Assets and Investments   74
Conclusion   75

Chapter 13. Climbing the Ladder and Putting It All Together   **77**

Action 1   77
Action 2   78
Action 3   79
Action 4   79
Hypothetical Case Studies   79
    Case Study A   79
    Possible Recommendations   80
    Case Study B   81
    Preliminary Comments   81
    Recommendations   82
Conclusion   82
    Remember . . .   83

Appendix A. Business Entity Checklist   **85**

Appendix B. LLC Explanation   **87**

Appendix C. Post-Incorporation Memorandum   **91**

Appendix D. Post-Organization Memorandum (For LLC)   **95**

Appendix E. Why Use Family Limited Liability Companies?   **99**

Appendix F. Asset Protection and Marital Planning   **103**

Appendix G. Bullet-Proofing Your Corporation   **107**

Appendix H. For Whom the Bell Toll   **109**

Appendix I. How to Avoid Veil-Piercing   **111**

Appendix J. The Nevada Asset Protection Trust   **115**

Appendix K. Putting Personal Residences into an FLP or FLCC: A No-No   **117**

Index   **119**

About the Author   **123**

Preface

The one constant over the many years of my practice and among the hundreds of different clients I have served is the imbalance between, on the one hand, their profound concern regarding Asset Protection, and on the other, their lack of understanding of how to implement it.

The purpose of this book is to provide readers with a straightforward and elementary understanding of what Asset Protection really is and how it can be effectively implemented by taking various steps—like rungs on a ladder. By reading this book, you as readers are initiating the process of protecting the assets you have worked so hard to build and preserve. It is, in essence, the beginning of your journey in setting up this hypothetical ladder. The goal of this discussion is to give you enough basic information to take the all-important next step in implementing your Asset Protection plan, and help you truly climb the ladder of success.

Over the years, I have represented hundreds of small business owners, physicians, professionals, corporate executives, and real estate investors. My practice has centered on meeting my clients' needs in the areas of Estate, Business, Asset Protection and Real Estate Planning. In addition, because of my substantial Estate Planning practice, I have also had extensive experience in Probate and Trust Administration.

Because most of these areas of the law are closely connected and become intertwined in the lives of my clients, it is important for them to have an integrated plan with respect to the protection, preservation, and transfer of their assets. That is why I have developed the concept of "The Ladder of Success"—a multi-tiered approach to addressing our clients' concerns and needs. Asset Protection Planning really is like a ladder: Such planning is multi-tiered and works together as a whole to bring an individual to a higher level of protection. Some of the steps of the ladder may not be relevant for each client, but for most professionals, almost all of the tiers are worthy of consideration and review.

The Ladder of Success is focused specifically on Asset Protection Planning and is designed to help all types of clients preserve and protect their assets during their lifetimes so they can be transferred in the most tax-saving and efficacious manner to the next generation.

Focus

Now, about the readers: I decided to write this book because of the tremendous need that business owners, physicians, other professionals, corporate executives, and real estate investors have with respect to protecting and preserving their assets. These individuals have worked hard and devoted tremendous time, effort, and capital in building up their estates. In the process, they have provided great services to our society. They have employed many people, they have paid taxes, and they have contributed significantly to the well-being of their clients and customers. They have made a difference and continue to do so with their creativity, energy, and business focus. These are people like you, who deserve respect, gratitude, and the happiness and peace of mind that come with knowing that their legacies are secure, that they can preserve and maintain their estates and pass them on to future generations.

In some small way, I hope this book can help them accomplish their goals and objectives—it is my way of thanking them for all they have given to society.

Introduction

Asset Protection Planning

Business persons have always been concerned about the exposure of their personal assets to claims against their businesses. Certainly, protecting one's assets from the myriad risks involved in business and personal financial planning is not a novel objective or planning idea. The corporate form of business entity, with its shield of limited liability, has been invoked by professionals for centuries to protect those personal resources. Over the last few decades, expanding theories of liability and the proliferation of litigation have given increased emphasis to Asset Protection Planning to the extent that it is now a well-recognized area of practice. It certainly comes within the concept of lifetime Estate Planning—involving the protection and conservation of accumulated wealth or asset base.

Shield of Liability

Business owners, physicians, and real estate investors must always be extremely concerned about potential liability against their personal assets, arising from the operation of the business or ownership of the real estate. Entities such as Corporations, Limited Liability Companies, and Limited Partnerships exist in part to prevent this potential personal liability.

- Corporations are formed to operate businesses and shield the corporate owner from personal liability against creditors of the business.

- Limited Liability Companies (LLCs) and Limited Partnerships (LPs) generally provide the necessary shield of liability for real estate investments; at the same time, they create favorable and flexible tax consequences because they are pass-through entities for income tax purposes.
- In addition, the potential limitation of the Charging Order remedy to creditors makes LLCs and LPs even more attractive and practical for business operators and real estate owners. (See Chapter 8 for more details regarding the Charging Order remedy.)

For clarity's sake, I will present an example of a typical business situation. Richard and his wife, Becky, own a small distribution business. They import products and distribute them on a wholesale basis to retail outlets. They have formed a corporation as the business entity for their distribution and operation. The office and warehouse that houses the distribution business is owned in an LLC, which they also own. The LLC then leases the premises to the distribution corporation. The corporation shield provides protection for Richard and Becky's non-business personal assets: creditors of the corporation can only seek redress from the corporation, and cannot normally attack the personal assets of the couple. The LLC provides protection to Richard and Becky's personal assets with respect to claims against the real estate itself. Richard and Becky were smart to segregate the real estate from the business operations and place the real estate in a separate liability-protected entity. In this way, a claim against the business will not necessarily impact the warehouse and offices inside the LLC. Moreover, a claim against the real estate will not necessarily impact the business operations inside the corporation and cannot normally be asserted against the other personal assets of Richard and Becky.

In June 2014, the US Supreme Court ruled in the case of *Clark v. Ramker* that an IRA (Individual Retirement Account) inherited from another is not a protected "retirement fund" and thus is subject to creditor's claims in bankruptcy. What this means is that unless the beneficiary of an inherited IRA is the resident of a state that specifically exempts inherited IRAs from creditors, such as Alaska, Florida, Missouri, or Texas, the inherited IRA will not be protected from bankruptcy. It may also be that except in those few states, an inherited IRA will also be available to satisfy non-bankruptcy creditors. Accordingly, it is advisable that an individual name a Trust design specifically for the purpose of being the beneficiary of his/her IRA and other retirement plans. The individual can thus ensure that the inherited IRA is protected from creditors regardless of the residence of the beneficiary.

Obviously, Richard and Becky are going to have liability insurance for the corporation and its business operations, as well as for the LLC and the real estate it possesses. However, there is always the danger that the claim is either outside the

> **NOTE**
>
> As our society has become more litigious, assent protection planning has become vitally important to business owners, real estate investors, physicians, and many other professionals.

scope of insurance coverage or that it may exceed the policy limits. On the other hand, the good news is that the corporation will provide substantial protection for Richard and Becky's personal assets against business claims, and the LLC will provide substantial protection for their personal assets for claims against the real estate and the LLC. During the remainder of this chapter and throughout other chapters, we will continue to refer to Richard and Becky's situation (the "Richard and Becky Fact Situation") as a way of better understanding planning techniques, strategies and implementation.

Inside and Outside Creditors

In Asset Protection Planning, creditors are often characterized as either "Inside" or "Outside".

Inside Creditors

Inside Creditors are those creditors whose claims are directed against the business operation or real estate operated and owned inside a separate business entity.

If the entity involved can withstand any piercing attack to its liability veil, then the creditor is limited to remedies against the assets within or inside the entity itself. For example, if a person who falls or slips at an apartment house owned by a properly structured and maintained LLC, that person only has the right to assert the claim against the LLC itself. The members and the managers of the LLC have no personal liability to the Inside Creditor, assuming that the LLC can stand up to any attacks of piercing the liability veil. We will further discuss protecting real estate assets by the utilization of LLCs in Chapter 8.

Most business operations and real estate investments utilizing a corporation or an LLC have liability insurance to protect against Inside Creditors. Business owners and real estate investors should carefully review their liability insurance policies to ensure that their coverage is adequate in both scope and amount. Unfortunately, there are many claims that fall outside of the parameters of the policy either with respect to coverage or policy limits.

As an example of an "Inside Debt" in the Richard and Becky Fact Situation referred to above, if a creditor of the distribution company were to make a claim about a faulty product distributed by Richard and Becky's corporation, that claim should theoretically only be against the corporation itself; Richard and Becky's personal assets and their real estate in the LLC should be protected from that claim. The claim would be an "Inside Debt" in the parlance of Asset Protection Planning, and this separation of assets into different entities would enable Richard and Becky to protect their property. Inside Debts are shielded by proper liability-protected structures.

TIP

Asset Protection Planning needs to account for potential claims against the business or real estate operation and those potential claims directed against the owner personally. The protection structure should be designed to limit personal liability.

Outside Creditors

Outside Creditors are those creditors whose claims are outside of the scope of the business entity and are generally asserted against the business or real estate owner personally. This could happen in the following circumstances:

- In some instances, these claims are closely connected to the business itself. This is the case with many service providers and professionals; they cannot escape personal liability by operating within a liability-protected entity because, as professionals and service providers, they are individually liable for their business-practice-related claims.
  - For example, physicians, lawyers, CPAs, engineers, and architects are personally liable for their malpractice regardless of the fact that they may be doing business in a professional corporation.
- Other examples of claims against individuals that do not come within the protection of the liability-protected entity include liability arising from auto accident claims and other personal (or "tort") claims above and beyond the scope of insurance coverage.
- Other claims may also include breach of contract claims for personal loans, guarantees, and other contractual obligations.

An example of an Outside Debt could be this: in the Richard and Becky Fact Situation, if Richard was at fault in an automobile accident, he would have personal liability which would (hopefully, but not necessarily) be covered by his insurance. If damages exceeded the covered amount, then Richard's creditor would attack both his business assets and his other personal assets for satisfaction of the claim. An alternative scenario would be: if Richard and his business operations encounter financial problems—and Richard and Becky default on a loan they have personally guaranteed—the financial institution would be able to seek redress against them personally. This would then be an "Outside Debt" in Asset Protection parlance.

A Comprehensive Example

In order to better understand the foregoing concepts, another case study will be helpful (though these terms are more specifically explained in subsequent chapters): Scott is a licensed architect with a successful architectural practice. He and his wife, Sophia, own three rental properties, and Scott has a limited partnership interest in the LP that owns the building where his offices are located. Scott interacts with several other professionals in the building in the course of providing his services. Scott and Sophia are the parents of three minor children, but have only taken a few basic Estate Planning steps. Obviously, because of the three minor children, Scott and Sophia are very concerned about Estate and Asset Protection Planning. They realize that not only are they at risk as a couple, but the three children are also substantially at risk because of their dependence on Scott and Sophia. What are some of the problems Scott and Sophia face? Here are several of the most important items they need to address:

1. Scott's Architectural Practice and the Ramifications of Operating as the Sole Proprietor

Because Scott interacts with other professionals, he should probably think of incorporating his practice. Although the incorporation will not provide a complete shield against his malpractice liability, it will help to protect Scott against potential liability of his associates and other building providers. This is the first level of protection every business owner and professional should address. We will discuss this area as the first step of The Ladder of Success in Chapter 5.

2. Estate Planning

Scott and Sophia should address some basic Estate Planning needs. They own several assets, and should anything happen to either one of them, they would need Wills with executors and guardians for their children. They need a Living Trust for their residence and other assets. They need Healthcare Powers of Attorney, Durable Powers of Attorney and other basic Estate Planning documents. These will be addressed in Chapter 6.

3. Exemption and Marital Planning

Scott and Sophia should examine different creditor exemptions and title their property in the manner most likely to provide Asset Protection. This may involve some Marital Planning and Marital Settlement Agreements that will be discussed in more detail in Chapter 7.

4. Liability-Protected Entities

Scott and Sophia own rental properties that can be exposed to claims either outside the scope of insurance coverage or beyond the insurance limits. Accordingly, Scott and Sophia should strongly consider placing these rental properties in LLCs to limit the liability to the property itself. This area will be discussed in more detail in Chapter 8 as Step Four of The Ladder of Success.

5. Domestic Asset Protection Trusts

Next, Scott and Sophia should definitely consider setting up a Domestic Asset Protection Trust. The combination of this Trust with the LLC Member Interest can provide superior protection against creditors' claims. This will be discussed in Chapter 9.

6. Offshore Planning

If Scott and Sophia have the inclination and the necessary liquidity, they might consider Offshore Asset Protection Trusts. This is, perhaps, the ultimate form of Asset Protection Planning for most individuals. However, going offshore is not for everybody. There are significant benefits, but the offshore experience is generally limited to those individuals who have substantial liquidity that can be placed offshore and/or have international connections of some form or another. This will be discussed in more detail in Chapter 10.

7. Advanced Estate Planning

Finally, there may be some advanced Estate Planning techniques that Scott and Sophia should consider. These include, but are not limited to, the following:

- The Irrevocable Life Insurance Trust (ILIT)
- The Grantor Retain Annuity Trust (GRAT)
- Sales to an Intentionally Defective Grantor Trust
- The Qualified Personal Residence Trust (QPRT)

These techniques will be discussed in Chapter 11.

8. Just What the Doctor Ordered

In Chapter 12, I have provided some special techniques and strategies for physicians and dentists. These service professionals face unique challenges and have their own particular issues as healthcare providers. All the other chapters in this book are also relevant to physicians and dentists; several of the case studies included throughout the book involve physicians. Chapter 12, however, specifically addresses physicians and dentists and their unique needs and requirements for Asset Protection Planning Services.

9. Putting It All Together

In Chapter 13, we will put it all together. We will give several case studies and explain how different tax situations can be analyzed and how design plans can be strategically developed to meet the needs and objectives of the individuals involved.

CHAPTER

2

Why Plan? The Need for Asset Protection

The Reasons

Over the last few decades, expanding theories of liability and the great proliferation of litigation have given increased emphasis to Asset Protection Planning. Potential liability is now a major concern to doctors, lawyers, business owners and other professionals of high net worth. Why is there such an increased liability exposure? The reasons are varied and somewhat obvious, but it is wise to examine them in greater detail.

1. Victim-Oriented Society

First of all, we now live in a victim-oriented society. There is a strong societal tendency to blame misfortune and general ills on some specific person or entity.

We are mere mortals; there are many instances of misfortune that occur on a daily and almost routine basis as a result of the imperfect world in which we live. Accidents happen, things get forgotten, mistakes are made, and sometimes things just go wrong. In the past, society recognized these unfortunate occurrences as a part of life. But over the past few decades, some people have developed a strong tendency to assign blame on someone or something instead of accepting the situation as a part of life.

This victim-oriented philosophy is based to some extent on the division of the "haves" and the "have nots." Victims of some of these misfortunes tend to place the blame on those who they perceive have more than them. While some of this blame may be properly directed, it clearly should not act as an excuse for or an impediment of proper behavior. It should also not impede someone from assuming individual financial responsibility for his or her own particular situation, nor for the good and ill-fortune that befalls him or her.

This victim-oriented philosophy, when combined with certain other factors and the "have" and "have nots" perception, has greatly contributed to the astounding proliferation of plaintiff-driven lawsuits.

2. Plaintiff Lawyers

Another substantial reason for expanding liability claims is the financial remuneration available to plaintiff lawyers who pursue their victim's claims. Most of the plaintiff lawyers take cases on a contingency basis; the victims don't personally pay to initiate and sustain the claims. The lawyers who take on these cases are willing to finance them because of the possibility of a pot of gold waiting in the form of extensive jury verdicts at the end of the case. The juries may be composed of individuals who believe in the victim-oriented rationale of some of the "have nots", and therefore see no problem in redistributing the wealth of professionals and business owners to the victim. The lawyers are driven by this strong financial potential and realize that the way to their own financial gain is to vigorously pursue these types of claims.

3. Expanding Theories of Liability

Courts are a reflection of society, and as the victim-oriented philosophy has established itself even more concretely, the courts, under pressure from aggressive plaintiff lawyers, have greatly expanded theories of liability against business owners, physicians, and other professionals of high net worth. The opportunist plaintiff lawyers who have advocated these expanding theories argue that as a result of litigation, legitimate victims have been compensated, and negligent practices have been eliminated—or at least rightfully punished and curtailed. The problem is that the plaintiff lawyers and juries apparently do not yet know when enough is enough or when enough should be nothing.

4. Deep-Pocket Theory

Another contributing factor is the Deep-Pocket Theory inherent with the "haves" and "have nots" syndrome. The rationale is that if someone has some wealth, then it really does not hurt them to extract a portion of it to compensate an alleged victim and to correct a so-called impropriety or act of negligence. With the exponential use of litigation, defendants with some financial means are tempted to settle even spurious claims in order to mitigate legal costs and eliminate the time and inconvenience involved with litigation.

5. Increased Notoriety

The final factor is the notoriety that all of these plaintiffs' actions receive. We are in a very transparent society, with the Internet, television, radio, and newspapers providing instantaneous and widely circulated news. The publicity that surrounds the awarding of huge jury verdicts greatly intensifies and increases the so-called victim's desire for compensation. The publicity is fuel for the plaintiffs' fire which becomes, accordingly, almost out of control in its incendiary ravage into the deep pockets of those blessed with assets and property.

Who are the Victims of Lawsuit Onslaughts? Who Needs to Protect and Defend their Amassed Assets and Properties?

- Doctors, dentists, lawyers, CPAs, architects, engineers, and other professionals subject to claims of malpractice and negligence
- Potential recipients of substantial inheritances from parents or other family members
- Business owners who might be subjected to personal liability as a result of the expanding theories of liability imposed by courts and statutes such as sexual and age discrimination, sexual harassment, and other tort claims
- Sellers' of business operations who are subjected to claims of fraud and nondisclosure when buyer's remorse sets in
- Individuals with high-risk businesses, such as waste, refuse and other businesses that impact the environment
- Any business individuals dealing with investors who may become disgruntled if the investment turns sour
- Individuals who have to sign personal guarantees and bonds, i.e., contractors and other business owners
- Officers and directors of public companies who face personal liability as a result of such cases as Enron and other related claims
- Owners of boats, airplanes, or extreme vehicles
- Real estate investors and owners
- Successful independent contractors who are at or near the top of a multi-level marketing or distribution program who have liability exposure from disgruntled, envious, and unsuccessful independent contractor underlings in their marketing and distributions systems
- Celebrities, high-net-worth and high-visibility individuals
- Wealthy spouses in a second marriage
- Children of wealthy individuals
- Almost anyone who has assets or property and who is involved in a serious automobile or other type of accident resulting in personal injury

Creditors, Discovery and Remedies

The fact that there are so many potential creditors' claims that can be asserted is only one side of the proverbial coin. The other side is the tremendous arsenal of creditor remedies that can be enforced once a claim turns into a judgment. Let us briefly map out the road a creditor would take in order to obtain and enforce the judgment.

The typical process begins when the facts giving rise to a claim occur. If a claim is contractual in nature, the claim arises when the alleged contract is breached or there is a default. For example, if an individual borrows money and signs a promissory note, the claim actually arises when that person defaults on the payment of the note. If an individual causes an automobile accident, the claim arises when the accident occurs. If a service provider is subject to a claim of malpractice, the malpractice has normally occurred when he or she rendered the allegedly faulty professional services to the client or patient.

Once the claim is discovered, the creditor normally issues a demand for compensation. Often, when it comes to a more complicated claim or a malpractice claim, the amount of damages cannot immediately be determined. The creditor then files a complaint and asks for damages either in a set amount or an amount to be proved later at court. Once the lawsuit is filed, the defendant must retain an attorney and file an answer to the lawsuit in the proper legal form. If the defendant fails to properly respond, the plaintiff will be able to obtain a default judgment. This eliminates the defendant's right to defend and contest the lawsuit claims. In this circumstance, the plaintiff would then have to prove the amount of his or her damages before the court, but the defendant would not have the right to contest the evidence of the amount.

> Hiding assets can be a crime. The point of Asset Protection is to create barriers that make it difficult for a plaintiff to access your wealth.

NOTE

If the defendant retains an attorney and files the necessary response, the lawsuit would then go into the Discovery Phase. In this phase, the plaintiff and defendant demand answers to written questions or interrogatories, as well as subpoena documents and records from each other or third parties who have information relative to the claim. Dispositions or formal recorded interviews with lawyers asking probing questions of the parties also takes place at this time. During Discovery and at its completion, there are opportunities for mediation either binding or non-binding, in order to settle the case and reduce legal fees and the risk of high judgments.

Once the Discovery process is completed—and assuming that mediation or court-enforced settlement hearings are unfruitful—then the matter is set for trial either before a jury or before the judge sitting alone. Most plaintiffs prefer jury trials because juries are likely to award much higher judgments than a judge would. If the plaintiff is successful at obtaining the judgment, then the plaintiff will immediately attempt to enforce the judgment. At this point, he or she may demand a judgment debtor examination, wherein debtor defendants are obligated (under penalty of perjury) to disclose all of their assets and sources of income. As we will see in Chapter 3, there are provisions in the law that prevent a potential debtor from transferring his or her assets to related parties in an attempt to avoid creditor claims. Accordingly, the plaintiff will ultimately prevail in uncovering all of the defendant's assets and sources of income. If the defendant has properly planned, even though the plaintiff knows about these assets and sources of income, there would be substantial barriers in place that would prevent the plaintiff from reaching the assets. These barriers give the judgment debtor much more leverage in working out a settlement with the creditor than if no planning and no

Asset Protection structure were involved. Once the plaintiff knows the judgment debtor's assets and sources of income, he or she can file judgment liens against the debtor's property, can attempt to garnish wages and other sources of income, and can attack many kinds of assets. At this point, the plaintiff may also file fraudulent conveyance actions against transferees of the debtor's property—such as relatives and friends who did not pay sufficient fair market value for such assets. The fraudulent transfer law is discussed in more detail in the next chapter.

The point that should be understood here is that because of the ability of the plaintiff to interview and demand information from the judgment debtor under penalty of perjury, the judgment debtor really cannot hide assets without committing a felony and going to jail. However, there are proper planning structures that can be implemented to provide significant barriers to plaintiff's remedies, and some can even render the remedies toothless. The critical element here is proper planning and preparation in advance, which obviously includes not only devising and developing an Asset Protection strategy, but also properly implementing it.

The Limitations

Fraudulent Transfer Law

It is not uncommon for a debtor, in an effort to protect his or her property from creditors, to attempt to transfer assets for little or no consideration to a relative or close friend with an underlying understanding that once the creditor's claims become stale or are eliminated, the transferee friend or relative will give the assets back to the debtor. Obviously, if there wasn't some limitation on this type of activity with accompanying creditor recourse, many creditors would never be able to enforce their judgments.

In order to address this transfer problem and protect the rights of creditors, the Statute of Elizabeth was passed in jolly old England back in 1571. The statute was the codification of the then-existing common law of England; it provided that all conveyances and transfer of property made with the intention of "delaying, hindering or defrauding creditors" or others would be completely void and of no effect. In 1918, several of the United States—through the National Conference of Commissioners on Uniform State Laws—issued what has now become The Uniform Fraudulent Conveyance Act (the UFCA). Most states have now either adopted and retained the UFCA or have adopted the Uniform Fraudulent Transfers Act (UFTA), issued in 1984. The states of California, Florida, Texas and others have adopted the UFTA. New York and a few other states have retained the UFCA as law.

Basically, under either the UFCA or the UFTA, a debtor cannot transfer assets if the principal reason is to prevent present or future creditors from gaining access to these assets. The language of "delaying, hindering or defrauding creditors" is still relevant. Under the UFTA, fraudulent transfers occur in one or both of two basic situations: (1) actual intent (smoking gun or badges of fraud); or (2) insolvency plus transfer for less than reasonably equivalent value. In analyzing fact situations in which a creditor is attempting to set aside a transfer as fraudulent, the court looks for a variety of salient features that have come to be known as "badges of fraud". If the court finds some or even just a few of these badges present, then the court may allow the creditor to set aside the transfer and force the transferee to disgorge the asset back to the debtor, while at the same time allowing the creditor to attach it and execute on it for satisfaction of the creditor's judgment. Some of these badges of fraud are as follows:

- Transfer to an insider such as a relative or friend
- Retention by the debtor of possession or control of the asset
- A concealment of the asset
- The potential for or existent threat of a suit
- The transfer of most of the debtor's assets
- The timing of such a transfer: whether the transfer occurred shortly before or shortly after a substantial debt was incurred

The other test involves whether or not the transfer has made the debtor insolvent. To determine whether the debtor is insolvent for purposes of the fraudulent transfer law, the debtor's assets are added up, and any assets that are exempt under the law are subtracted. Also added in is the amount of any insurance coverage that may be applicable to the claim in question. From this sum total, we must also subtract the known liabilities and any reasonably anticipated liabilities. This gives us a net worth figure for fraudulent transfer purposes.

> One of the most common errors is to wait until a potential problem arises before creating an Asset Protection structure, a situation which exposes the individual to fraudulent transfer law violations. PLAN EARLY!

CAUTION

For example, if John White is a practicing physician with assets (including a personal residence) worth $3 million, and malpractice insurance coverage of $1 million, and he lives in California where the homestead exemption is $75,000.00, then his total assets for purposes of the fraudulent transfer law would be $3,925,000.00. If he has liabilities of $1 million, and if the threatened lawsuit for malpractice is a potential $3 million jury award, then John's net worth for fraudulent transfer purposes would be negative.

Some of the planning techniques used in order to generate a reasonably equivalent value for the transfer process are:

- Traditional sales
- Installment sales
- Private annuities
- Factoring arrangements

These techniques usually require sophisticated and specialized legal counseling. It is recommended that any individuals facing creditors' claims should obtain competent legal counsel before attempting to enter into any transfer transaction; otherwise, it could be deemed a fraudulent transaction. These transactions or transfers, otherwise called fraudulent conveyances, are attempts to avoid or hinder creditors by transferring assets from the debtor to a third party. They are subject to being set-aside or voided by the court.

If we made up a spectrum of fraudulent conveyance, illustrating the probability of a fraudulent finding, it would look as follows:

Safe Haven?	1.Facts Occur	2.Claim Asserted	3.Lawsuit Filed	4.Trial Preparation	5.Trial	6.Judgment

Figure 3.1. The Matsen Spectrum of Fraudulent Conveyance Applicability

The farther to the right on the spectrum an individual is when he or she transfers property, the more likely it is that the transfer will be deemed fraudulent for purposes of the fraudulent conveyance law. If a creditor has already obtained a judgment against the debtor, and the next day the debtor transfers his or her assets, the transfer is going to be highly suspect and likely will be set aside. At the same time, however, there may be some business and Estate Planning transfers that would withstand fraudulent conveyance scrutiny because they are not done to delay, hinder or defraud creditors, but have a strong enough independent business or Estate Planning purpose (and have within the transaction the receipt of reasonably equivalent value).

One of the important factors of the fraudulent conveyance law that most professionals (and even some attorneys) do not understand is this:

- For purposes of fraudulent conveyance analysis, the creditor status occurs at the time that the facts occur giving rise to the claim, not when the claim is actually asserted or the lawsuit is initiated.

For example, the creditor-favored status under the fraudulent transfer law happens when the individual signs the contract or guarantee, not when the contract or guarantee is breached. Similarly, the favorable creditor status comes into play on the date the surgeon or other professional commits the malpractice, not when the malpractice is discovered or its coinciding claim is made.

What this highlights and emphasizes is that **advance planning is critical**. Looking back at the spectrum of fraudulent conveyance applicability (Figure 3.1 above), the best place to be is in the potentially Safe Haven period before the facts actually occur that give rise to the claim. If the transfers and Asset Protection structure are instituted in advance of the action giving rise to the claim, then the likelihood of a fraudulent conveyance argument prevailing is extremely remote.

To better illustrate the application of the fraudulent transfer law, let us assume that John White is being sued by a financial institution for default relative to a $350,000 loan. John's only asset of any real value is a condominium he rents out that is valued at $200,000. John talks this over with his brother, Dave, and then deeds the Condo over to Dave. Once the creditor obtains judgment against John, the creditor then subpoenas John to attend a creditor examination in court where John is required to testify under penalty of perjury. The creditor then asks John whether he or anyone acting under his control or direction or with his knowledge or consent has transferred, assigned or conveyed any asset to any person within the last 24 months. John either has to commit perjury, which is a felony, or he has to tell the creditor about the conveyance of his condo to his brother, Dave. The creditor would then institute an action against John and Dave requesting an order by the court that (1) Dave be forced to disgorge the asset back to John and, at the same time, (2) the creditor be given a lien on the Condo to execute in partial satisfaction of its judgment.

Obviously, whenever Asset Protection Planning takes place, the fraudulent conveyance law has to be examined. Once again, the sooner really is the better when it comes to planning. Unfortunately, many professionals, business owners and real estate investors wait until it is too late to structure the best plan. There may still be some steps which can be taken after a creditor appears, but the best planning can only occur before the facts that give rise to the creditor claims happen.

Bankruptcy

Bankruptcy is not a viable option for clients who have substantial assets and who want to retain as many of those assets as possible. One reason for this is that the bankruptcy courts and the appointed receivers and Trustees therein have more power and much more flexibility in enforcing judgments over the debtor than the normal state court jurisdictions.

There are a few basic bankruptcy considerations that should be noted in our limited discussion:

- First, in bankruptcy, any transfer within two years before the date of filing made with the actual intent to hinder, delay or defraud any present or future creditor may be voided by the bankruptcy court.
- In addition, if there are preferences made to a creditor prior to filing bankruptcy, such preference can possibly be set aside.
- Moreover, an amendment was added to the Bankruptcy Act—the Talent Amendment—allowing a special 10-year avoidance period for a transfer made with actual intent to hinder, delay or defraud a present or future creditor if the transfer was made by the debtor to a Self-Settled Trust or similar device. A Self-Settled Trust is one set up by the individual to benefit himself or herself. At first, this would appear to be a major problem in setting up any Asset Protection structure. However, the intent has to be "actual," and this most likely means that it has to be related to an existing creditor claim. Therefore, domestic and offshore, Self-Settled Trusts can still be outside the purview of the Talent Amendment. We should note,

however, that a recent case in the Bankruptcy Court in Alaska (*The Mortensen Case*) held that the "intent" can be found for future creditors if other badges of fraud (factors casting a negative intent on the maker of the Trust) are present.

The bottom line is that bankruptcy should only be considered when there are no other options or when there are little or no assets in the debtor's estate. If the estate has assets, it normally makes sense for the debtor to stay out of bankruptcy and try to work things out with the creditors, utilizing only the threat of bankruptcy.

Money Laundering and Other Criminal Statutes

The Money Laundering Control Act was originally enacted as part of the Anti-Drug Abuse Act of 1986, but it has been expanded into the areas of bank fraud and similar activities. The Act talks about specified unlawful activity. It is a crime to knowingly be involved in any transaction where the source of funds is derived from an unlawful activity. Attorneys, CPAs, and Trust officers will want to exercise proper due diligence to make sure that any funds involved in Asset Protection Planning do not come within the purview of the Money Laundering Control Act.

There is also the RICO Act, which applies to racketeer influence, and corrupt organizations and funds derived from racketeering activities. The Patriot Act also contains anti-money-laundering elements. Following the terrorist attacks of September 11, 2001, the United States and other countries have applied the Patriot Act and other types of legislation. Thus, banks and other financial institutions are now much more on guard and apply higher standards of scrutiny with respect to opening bank accounts and obtaining the proper due diligence information about account holders. Accordingly, it is not uncommon for a prospective client to have to disclose the source of his or her income and assets and to provide basic verification information. Legitimate professional and business persons need not have any concern with respect to the foregoing, but nevertheless have to disclose much more personal information than they have in the past.

CHAPTER

4

The Ladder of Success

The Multi-Tiered Approach

Over the years, I have had the opportunity of presenting several continuing education courses for other attorneys in the areas of Estate and Asset Protection Planning, as well as business entity formation—specifically Limited Liability Companies. I have the privilege of belonging to WealthCounsel, which is an association of more than 3,300 attorneys nationwide who practice in the Estate Planning area. I have been involved in structuring and preparing several education courses for WealthCounsel and its members. During that process, with the input of a few other WealthCounsel principals and members, I have developed a multitiered approach to Estate and Asset Protection Planning that I call *The Wealth Strategies Counsel Ladder of Success*, and is displayed in Figure 4.1.

This is the ladder introduced in Chapter 1. Each step on the ladder—or level of strategy—provides immediate Asset Protection and Estate Planning benefits. Some or all levels of the complete ladder will be applicable to every business owner, physician, other professional and real estate investor, depending on the individual state of the career development and net worth. As discussed in Chapter 1, the diagram below illustrates the steps on the ladder and the levels of strategy:

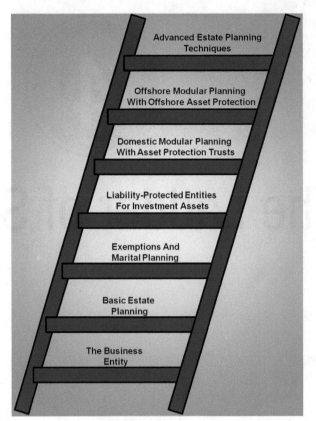

Figure 4.1. The Ladder of Success—Step-by-Step

Step One: The Business Entity

This level encompasses the individual's operating business, which is both the primary source of his or her income and the entity to which the business owner or professional gives the majority of his or her time. For example, if we are talking about a physician, it is his or her professional practice. If we are talking about a business person who owns and operates a restaurant, it is the restaurant operation. If we are talking about a business owner who owns and operates a small manufacturing company, it is the manufacturing operation itself.

There may be more than one entity involved with respect to the business operations, and the business operations themselves may be intertwined and closely connected with other assets and property of the business owner or professional. For example, the practicing physician may own all or a part of the medical building in which he or she practices. The medical building may be in another liability-protected entity, such as a Limited Liability Company, which leases the premises to the physician and the physician's professional corporation. A small business owner may own the restaurant building in which the restaurant operates and, again, most likely will lease the building to the corporation that operates the restaurant. We will discuss this step on the ladder more specifically in Chapter 5.

Step Two: Basic Estate Planning

Level Two involves basic Estate Planning for the professional or business owner. What do we mean by basic Estate Planning? We are talking about Wills, Revocable Living Trusts, Durable Powers of Attorney, Healthcare Powers of Attorney and Medical Record Release Authorization Forms. This is a basic level which should be addressed by almost everybody, but especially business owners, service professionals, and real estate investors. Basic Estate Planning will be discussed in more detail in Chapter 6.

Step Three: Exemptions and Marital Planning

This ladder level addresses the fact that there are several assets (classified as exemptions) that are protected from creditor attack and, normally, are also exempted from bankruptcy. They include homestead exemptions, insurance and annuities, and retirement plans.

Level Three on our Ladder also includes Marital Planning. This type of planning involves the consideration of retitling assets to the nonworking spouse, who is less likely to be at risk. We will go through some of this planning and utilizing in Chapter 7, and also discuss exemptions.

Step Four: Liability-Protected Entities for Investment Assets

This level of strategy involves analyzing an individual's assets that fall outside of his or her business operations. This may include rental-income-producing real estate, securities, and other types of financial accounts and other properties. Strong consideration should be given to placing most, if not all, of these other assets into liability-protected entities such as Limited Liability Companies. In Chapter 8, we will examine this strategy in more detail through case studies.

Step Five: Domestic Modular Planning with Asset Protection Trusts

This strategy combines the utilization of liability-protected entities (discussed in Step Four of the ladder) with the utilization of Domestic Asset Protection Trusts. Thirteen states have now adopted favorable legislation providing exceptions to the general rule that Self-Settled Trusts do not ensure Asset Protection. These states have passed enabling legislation that generates substantial protection against creditors' claims for persons creating these Trusts. In Chapter 9, we will further explain Domestic Asset Protection Trusts and the Modular Planning that goes with them.

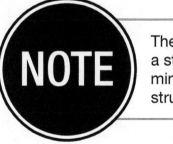

The Ladder of Success provides a structured process for determining the right Asset Protection structure for every individual.

Step Six: Offshore Modular Planning with Offshore Asset Protection Trust

Much of the same strategy utilized in Domestic Planning is involved on this level of the ladder, but instead of assets being located domestically, they are placed offshore for even greater protection. Chapter 10 examines the benefits of going offshore and discusses the structures that are utilized to do so.

Step Seven: Advanced Estate Planning Techniques

These advanced techniques are relevant not only for Asset Protection, but also Estate Planning. Most of them involve estate tax savings and are beneficial with respect to passing assets to future generations without incurring significant estate tax charges. These techniques are discussed in more detail in Chapter 11.

Physician Planning

Chapter 12 focuses on several issues of Asset Protection Planning specific to physicians and dentists.

Putting It All Together

Chapter 13 will then put everything together—integrating all of the techniques on the Ladder and utilizing hypothetical case studies to help the reader understand how these techniques can be applicable.

The Multi-Tiered Modular approach is extremely beneficial, not only for purposes of implementing and structuring a plan, but also for understanding and initiating that plan.

The Ladder

When climbing a ladder, one must decide which rungs to use and which can be skipped. As we proceed up the ladder through the following chapters, it is critical to note that though these steps are the basics of Asset Protection, not all of them apply to each person's situation. By climbing the ladder step by step, we analyze the various strategies and techniques of planning in order for readers to determine their applicability to their own personal circumstances.

Step One on the Ladder

The Operating Business Entity

One of the first important decisions a business owner or practicing professional must address is selecting the proper form of business entity. This is a crucial decision because of its ongoing legal and tax consequences. Liability protection is the most important nontax consideration in the business-entity-selection process. Business owners need a shield or umbrella covering their business activities in order to protect their other non-business assets from liability exposure. These claims are the kinds of "Inside Debts" we defined in Chapter 1. They are the claims that are directed to and arise from the business operations itself. No prudent business owner in our litigious, deep-pocket-searching society can afford to operate without either incorporating or establishing a Limited Liability Company (LLC). The Sole Proprietorship or General Partnership mode of doing business is a thing of the past.

Let me give you an example. A few years ago, a Latino family that operated three Mexican restaurants as more or less a mom-and-pop type of operation was referred to our firm. They were basically facing two different kinds of claims: one, from a customer who allegedly slipped and fell at one of the restaurant locations, and another from a former employee who was alleging sexual harassment.

Unfortunately, the location at which the slip-and-fall incident occurred was not properly insured at the time because of an inadvertent oversight between the owners and the insurance broker. All three restaurant locations' assets were subject to liability from the customer's claim. If this entity had been incorporated instead of being operated as a proprietorship by the family, then only one restaurant might have been the subject of the claim, and the liability potential could have been greatly limited. We were able to successfully negotiate a settlement with respect to the suspicious slip-and-fall claim, and the family immediately set up three different corporations for the three different restaurant operations.

The sexual harassment claim was different because that was not only directed against the business entity, but against the owner himself. Accordingly, it was both an Inside Debt as a claim against the business, as well as an Outside Debt because it was a claim asserted personally against the owner. A judgment arising from this claim could have been substantial, but it was eventually settled on somewhat reasonable terms. (However, another one of our business clients had a sexual harassment claim that was only settled after the payment of thousands of dollars. Fortunately, that client had done some Asset Protection Planning, and the planning helped in reaching what could have otherwise been a disastrous settlement award.)

Getting back to our business owner, the question of whether or not to create a liability-shielded entity in which to operate the business or to "go bare," so to speak, and operate as a proprietorship or a General Partnership is a no-brainer. The business owner needs to either incorporate and operate as a corporation or set up an LLC and operate the business as an LLC.

It is not the author's intent, nor within the purview of this book, to delve in detail into the different forms of business operating entities. We will only briefly examine each of the different types of entities available, spending more time on S Corps and LLCs as they are the most popular and often the best business entity vehicle.

Generally, business owners will choose between the following six types of entities:

- Sole Proprietorship
- General Partnership
- Limited Partnership
- Corporation
- Limited Liability Company
- Limited Liability Partnership

Each of these entities has its own advantages and disadvantages.

Sole Proprietorship

The Sole Proprietorship is the simplest form of business organization. It is not itself a legal entity, but it refers to a natural person who owns and operates the business and is responsible for its debts. Since the individual is the one doing business, there is no State Charter or organizational document which has to be filed with any state agency in order for the Proprietorship to exist. In many states, a Fictitious Firm Name Statement will have to be filed where the business operates under a name different than the owner. The Sole Proprietorship reports its income and expenses for tax purposes on Schedule C of the individual form 1040 Federal Tax Return. The Proprietorship has the advantage of a simple formation, but also has the substantial disadvantage of unlimited liability against the business owner. It also creates problems for Estate Planning because the business terminates upon the death of the owner, and it is difficult to pass a Proprietorship business on to heirs. These disadvantages make the Proprietorship almost entirely unsatisfactory for most business operations.

General Partnership

A General Partnership is any business engaged in, for profit, by two or more business owners. In a sense, it is the default business entity classification that exists when joint business owners don't select another form of business entity. As a result, individuals doing business together may be deemed *de facto* partners with the obligations and liabilities of partners without actually entering into a written agreement regarding their relationship. A General Partnership can normally be set up without any form of state filing and usually does not require a State Charter to be a valid partnership. Normally, the Partnership business will have to file a Fictitious Firm Name Statement because it is not doing business under the name of a State-chartered entity. The disadvantages of a General Partnership include unlimited personal liability for partnership obligations and may also result in liability for one partner of another partner's debts and actions. It is also a problem entity for Estate Planning purposes. In the past, General Partnerships of real estate ownership were common. Currently, however, because of the disadvantages mentioned above, no properly advised individual owns real estate or operates a business in the General Partnership form.

The General Partnership files a Federal Income Tax Return, but the Partnership itself does not pay any taxes. The profits and losses are passed through to the individual partners by means of individual K-1 forms that are reported on the individual's personal tax return. For tax purposes, the Partnership form does provide for substantial flexibility in allocating profits and losses. However, that same flexibility can be obtained by utilizing liability-protected entities such as LLCs and Limited Partnerships that elect to be taxed as Partnerships.

Limited Partnership

Limited Partnerships consist of a General Partner who manages and operates the Partnership and various limited partners who are more or less passive investors. The Limited Partnership is typically a State-chartered entity and almost always has to have a written agreement delineating the duties and responsibilities of the General Partner and the Limited Partners. Properly drafted, the agreement provides a liability shield for the Limited Partners who are generally not liable for the debts of the Partnership except to the extent of their capital contributions. The Limited Partnership does file a Federal Tax Return, but like a General Partnership, no taxes are paid at the Partnership level; the individual partners receive K-1 forms, reflecting their share of the profits and losses of the Partnership. The principal disadvantage of the Limited Partnership is that the General Partner remains personally liable for the debts of the business. Accordingly, in order to shield the General Partner from personal liability, another entity, either a Corporation or an LLC, should be established to be the actual General Partner of the Limited Partnership. Because of the inconvenience and expense involved in setting up a second entity for liability protection for the General Partner, LLCs have become much more popular and are now generally utilized in the place of Limited Partnerships.

Limited Liability Company

The Limited Liability Company (LLC) provides the tax benefits of a Partnership as a pass-through tax entity while affording the members of the LLC the same kind of liability protection a corporation affords. The LLC is a State-chartered entity and is either taxed as a disregarded entity, if it is a sole-member LLC, or as a partnership if it is a multimember LLC. The LLC can be managed in two ways:

- Manager-managed, which provides much the same kind of management structure as a Limited Partnership (a General Partner and Limited Partners)
- Member-managed, which resembles the General Partnership form of management structure

The choice of the proper business entity is a vital first step to create a shield of protection for the business owner. For most owners, a C Corp or S Corp would be advisable.

In addition to providing protection against Inside Debts, the LLC also provides some additional protection with respect to Outside Debts in that the Charging Order is the principal remedy a creditor has with respect to going against the assets of the LLC. The Charging Order and utilization of LLCs will be discussed in much greater detail in Chapter 8.

Corporation

A Corporation is a separate legal entity that is State-chartered. It has its own separate identity, separate and apart from the shareholder owners who created it.

The corporate management structure is different from any of the other types of entities. The owner shareholders elect directors, after which the shareholders have little to do with the management of the corporation. The directors elect officers and make the major policy decisions of the corporation, both financial and business. The officers operate the business on a day-to-day basis. The shareholders become involved only with major transactions, such as the sale of substantially all of the assets of the corporation, liquidation, or dissolution of the corporation.

For tax purposes, a corporation is one of two types:

- A C Corporation, which is taxed as a completely separate entity from the shareholders
- An S Corporation (more formally known as a Subchapter S or Sub S Corporation), which is a pass-through tax entity similar to a Partnership

For legal purposes, there is no distinction between a C Corp and an S Corp.

The major advantage of a corporation is that it affords a shield of liability protecting the shareholder owners from claims against the business. It is a perpetual entity and is therefore a good vehicle for Estate Planning purposes.

The major disadvantage of a C Corporation with respect to tax considerations is the fact that a double tax can result on corporate profits. These profits are taxed at the corporate level and then, again, at the shareholder level if they are distributed to shareholders as dividends. Small, closely-held corporations whose owners are involved in the corporate business can avoid the problem of double taxation by taking out the profits as salaries. If they are passive investors, however, who do not work directly for the corporation, double taxation remains a major problem.

Because of the double-tax situation that occurs not only with the operating income of the business, but also upon the eventual sale of the business, the S Corporation is highly favored over the C Corporation. Most buyers of businesses do not want to buy the corporate stock or entity as a whole; they prefer to buy the assets. Accordingly, an S Corporation is a much better vehicle for exit strategy planning because it avoids the problem of the double tax that occurs upon the sale of assets of a C Corporation.

Limited Liability Partnership

A Limited Liability Partnership (LLP) is similar to a General Partnership with the added benefit of a corporate-style limited liability shield for its partners. The LLP is a relatively recent creation that affords the benefits of a limited liability for partners in law, accounting and architectural firms organized as General Partners. It is a State-chartered entity and is taxed like a Partnership.

Selecting the Proper Business Entity

Almost any business operation should be conducted in an entity providing a shield of liability. For most business owners, the C Corp or the S Corp are viable options. Most professionals also incorporate as a Professional Corporation and can gain some benefit of protection even though they may also have personal liability with respect to the professional services they render. The benefit of the Professional Corporation is that it provides a shield against the liability of others involved in the professional process. For example, the Professional Corporation may shield a doctor from certain malpractice claims against other physicians, clinics, or hospitals.

TIP

To maintain the integrity of the Asset Protection structure, there should be no co-mingling of personal and business expenses. To do so invites an attack by a claimant on the entity shield.

In conclusion, the operating business entity is a major tier on the Ladder of Success that must be addressed. With the corporation, there are corporate formalities that have to be maintained and updated, such as the preparation of Minutes and Resolutions. The LLC does not have the same compliance requirements, but must still be treated as a separate entity. Attached as Appendix A is a Business Entity Checklist that can prove very valuable for both lay persons and their advisors. Appendix B is a more complete explanation of the LLC. Appendix C is a Post-Incorporation Memorandum our law firm provides to its clients who have formed a corporation in California. Attached as Appendix D is a Post-Organization Memorandum we provide to our clients who have formed an LLC.

As the memorandums attached as Appendix C and D strongly emphasize, it is extremely critical that the integrity of the corporation and/or LLC be maintained. There can be no co-mingling of personal funds with the business funds. Personal expenses should not be paid out of the business-operating accounts. The owner, shareholder, or member should take a draw and pay personal expenses from their own personal bank accounts. Co-mingling of personal funds can be a major problem in attempting to defend against a piercing attack on the Corporate or LLC veil.

Step Two on the Ladder

Basic Estate Planning

The multi-tiered approach to overall planning for the business owner and professional has to include Estate Planning as an integral element. Estate Planning is essentially the process of preserving and protecting your assets and property, then anticipating and arranging for them to be passed on to the next generation in the most orderly manner possible. There are many purposes behind developing an Estate Plan:

- Preserve and grow your assets during life
- Eliminate uncertainties with respect to the disposition of assets at death
- Maximize the value of the assets you pass to the next generation by reducing death taxes and avoiding Probate

Estate Planning is basically the design and implementation of a plan that (1) will provide for individuals and their families if they become disabled and (2) will facilitate the transition of their property (including their business, professional practice, and investments) upon their death with a minimum of expense, delay, taxes, and unnecessary court intervention.

Foundational Documents

The foundational documents for Estate Planning include:

- Wills
- Trusts

- Beneficiary designations
- Powers of Attorney
- Healthcare Directives
- Gifting
- Special provisions for minor children and loved ones with special needs

We will briefly address each of these foundational documents below.

Will and Powers of Attorney

A Will is likely the most well understood of these documents. It provides for the appropriate distribution of assets at death. One of the most important parts of a Will is to name an executor who has the responsibility to collect and distribute assets and to administer the Estate. The Will provides for distribution of personal property such as furnishings, clothing, and other personal items that are not generally funded into the Trust. Another important appointment of the Will is for the guardian of minor children. Everyone who has minor children should have a Will in order to cover this important function.

Most business owners and professionals also need a Living Trust. In conjunction with a Living Trust, a Pour-Over Will is a type of Will utilized to incorporate the Trust by reference so the assets can be distributed according to provisions of the Trust. When we meet with clients to execute Estate Planning documents, I like to compare the size of the Trust document to the Will. The Will is usually just a few pages long in comparison to the dozens of pages of the Trust. This is because the Will actually incorporates the Trust by reference.

As stated above, one of the most important features of the Will is to name an executor who is responsible for the following:

- Marshalling together all of an individual's assets
- Paying off existing debts and expenses
- Carrying out the deceased's funeral and burial wishes
- Coordinating with the successor Trustee of the Living Trust relative to the preparation of any Estate Tax Return (Federal Form 706) and the preparation and payment of any income taxes during the year of death

A Power of Attorney is an authorization to act on someone else's behalf in a legal or business manner. A Durable Power of Attorney continues in place, even if the grantor becomes incapacitated. The Power of Attorney expires at death. When an Estate Plan is formulated, most people choose to have a Durable Power of Attorney—one broad enough to confer all the legal rights the individual himself or herself enjoys on a loved one or trusted friend. In this way, if the person becomes mentally incapacitated, the loved one or trusted friend can take care of all of the legal and financial matters on behalf of the incapacitated grantor.

NOTE

There are a multitude of documents involved in creating a proper Estate Plan. Seek out a qualified attorney to develop your Estate Plan and then review the plan regularly as your family and financial circumstances change.

Healthcare Directives or Medical Powers of Attorney

A Healthcare Directive or Medical Power of Attorney is utilized to enable the appointed agent to make decisions on behalf of the grantor. Typically, when an individual is injured or suffers some sickness that requires hospitalization or medical care, a Medical Power of Attorney or Healthcare Directive will be required by the medical provider. This is a necessity because the patient may become incapable of making decisions himself or herself, and the agent can then step into the shoes of the patient and authorize the medical provider to proceed with the necessary medical treatment. The Healthcare Directive also deals with the sensitive issues that occur when the grantor is in a vegetated state or irreversible coma, and it is appropriate for the agent to terminate the artificial means of keeping the patient alive. In addition to the Healthcare Directive or Medical Power of Attorney, an individual also needs to execute a Medical Records Release Form giving the agent authority to access the grantor's medical records. This is necessary even in the case of a spouse accessing the records of the other spouse, under the rules of Privacy promulgated by the HIPAA.

The Revocable Living Trust

A Living Trust is a legal document drafted by a qualified attorney that contains the makers' (the maker of the Trust is called the Trustor or Settlor) instructions for the disposal of his or her assets at death. Unlike a Will, a Living Trust avoids Probate—making the administration of an Estate at death much simpler and less expensive for the heirs. A Living Trust is just like setting up one's own family company that he or she controls and that continues on past his or her death to carry out dispositive wishes. The concept is very simple and avoids the expense and delay of court proceedings. Trustors retain control of the assets in the Trust because they are also the managers or Trustee of the Trust; they can do everything they could do before placing the assets in the Trust (such as buy and sell assets, change or even cancel the Trust and even file the same tax returns). Nothing but the names on the title changes with respect to the assets in the Trust.

Briefly, the primary benefits of a Living Trust are as follows:

- It avoids Probate at death
- It prevents court control of assets in case of incapacity
- It provides maximum privacy
- It can help reduce or eliminate estate taxes
- It can be changed or cancelled at any time
- It can protect dependents with special needs
- It brings all of the assets together under one plan for a more orderly disposition

The typical Living Trust, however, does not provide protection against creditors of the Trustor of the Trust. It can provide protection against creditors of that individual's heirs, but normally, it offers no protection whatsoever against his or her own creditors. That is why it is essential that business owners or professionals explore other means to protect their assets during their lifetimes, as explained in the following pages.

While a traditional Living Trust has numerous benefits, it does not provide protection against the creditors of the Trustor. Additional mechanisms must be put in place.

CAUTION

Most of our clients choose to set up a Revocable Living Trust (RLT) as part of their basic Estate Plan. However, setting up an RLT is not enough. In order for the Living Trust to be effective and carry out the instructions of the Trustor, it is important that the Trustor's assets be re-titled into the name of the Trust. This means an individual must change titles from his or her name into the name of the Trust on real estate (by deed recorded with the county recorder's office), as well as other titled assets such as stocks, bank accounts, business interests and other investments. No one should have a Trust prepared without having his or her assets properly re-titled into the name of the Trust. Individuals need to also change most beneficiary designations to their Trustee. These beneficiary designations include insurance, annuities, IRAs, pension plans, and other retirement programs. Re-titling assets into a Trust is commonly known as "funding" a Trust.

In most instances, the same person or couple who make the Trust as Trustors also serve as Trustees. Therefore, the Trustors (in their capacity as Trustees) continue to control the assets in their Trust during their lifetime.

A Trust must be properly funded because if an individual's assets are not held in the name of the Trust, they will not avoid Probate in spite of establishing the Trust. If we think of the Trust as a basket, we can see that the assets placed in the basket can be distributed according to the instructions of the Trust upon death of the Trustor. The assets inside the basket do not have to be probated; the Trustor's heirs will know what assets they own because they will be set forth on a schedule attached to the Trust. Almost all of one's assets—except personal property like clothing, furniture, and automobiles—should be put inside the Trust.

Obviously, any Estate Plan for a professional or business owner must take into account Exit Strategy Planning and Business Succession. Buy-sell agreements are critical; thus, the Estate Planning and Asset Protection process should always include Exit Strategy and Business Succession. Even as I am writing this book, I am assisting several clients in the important area of business succession. Some of these clients own family businesses and want their children to be involved in the business succession plan.

Other clients are in the process of setting up buy-sell arrangements with key employees. Still other business owners and professionals are building up their business or practice in a way that will make it more attractive for potential buyers. In any event, a key component of Estate Planning for the business owner and professional is an Exit Strategy and Business Succession Plan.

We will discuss more sophisticated Estate Planning strategies and techniques in Chapter 11. The foundation, of course, must be put in place. In short, the basic components of any well-structured Estate Plan involve the Revocable Living Trust and the Wills, Powers of Attorney, and Healthcare Directives that should accompany the establishment and design of the Trust.

One final word about Estate Planning: When choosing legal counsel, ensure your Estate Planning will not be neglected. For instance, we provide an Estate Planning Maintenance or Protection Program for our clients. This is an essential feature of our legal representation. Our Program involves the payment of a small annual fee by our clients, in exchange for which we provide unlimited telephone calls and estate review at no charge. We also advise our clients of any change in the laws that may impact their Estate Plan and keep them educated and up-to-date regarding any techniques or planning issues that may become relevant to their estate. We also have seminars for educating young adults in Estate management and Estate Planning. We value our continuing relationships with our clients, and our clients like the fact that we are protecting their interests.

TIP

Business owners should plan their exit strategy well in advance of when they wish to leave the business. In many cases, it makes sense to spend time and effort into enhancing the value of the business before seeking potential buyers.

CHAPTER

7

Step Three on the Ladder

Bankruptcy Considerations, Exemptions, and Marital Planning

Any discussion of Asset Protection Planning should include at least a brief examination of bankruptcy laws. Hopefully, this will never be an alternative for most business owners or professionals facing financial troubles. A Bankruptcy Judge has much broader and more liberal powers to reach debtors' assets than a State Court Judge; thus, for anyone who has assets, bankruptcy is not a very good option. It is important, however, to at least acknowledge the worst and plan accordingly.

There are various exemptions available under both bankruptcy laws and state creditor remedies that are important to consider. Moreover, there may be some Marital Planning that can enhance an Asset Protection structure. All of the above considerations will be addressed in this chapter.

Bankruptcy Considerations

Any discussion of bankruptcy must be undertaken with the understanding that estate domicile is very important. Bankruptcy law supersedes state law in most instances, but sometimes the bankruptcy court will defer to state law where there is no specific bankruptcy provision to the contrary. Any business owner or professional under attack by a creditor (where bankruptcy may be a consideration) should consult with local bankruptcy counsel to better understand bankruptcy ramifications.

As mentioned previously, generally, any transfer of assets to another entity or person within two years before the date of filing made with the actual intent to hinder, delay or defraud any present or future creditors may be voided by the bankruptcy court. This provision of the bankruptcy law is closely intertwined with

the fraudulent transfer law that was previously discussed in Chapter 3, though it is specific to bankruptcy court.

Also, as alluded to previously, under the Talent Amendment, a special 10-year avoidance period exists under the Bankruptcy Code; but, it only exists for a transfer made with actual intent to hinder, delay or defraud a present or future creditor if the transfer was made by the debtor to a Self-Settled Trust or similar device. (In Chapter 9, we will be discussing Domestic Asset Protection Trusts; these may come under the purview of the Talent Amendment as a Self-Settled Trust.) This provision of the Bankruptcy Code could possibly set aside a structure utilizing a Domestic Asset Protection Trust. However, almost all attorneys who deal in the Asset Protection Planning area agree that the requirement of "actual intent" must be present to trigger the application of the Talent Amendment to an Asset Protection Trust—as long as the Trust is entered into, and transfers of assets are made prior to the fact that gives rise to any substantial creditor claim. "Actual intent" requires a showing that the transfer was made specifically to avoid a particular creditor who was either in existence or was at least foreseeable at the time of the set-up of the Trust and the transfer of the assets therein. Some nationally recognized lawyers have argued that the Talent Amendment is a death knoll for Asset Protection Trusts. Other attorneys may disagree, but, manifestly, bankruptcy judges have very broad and sweeping powers, and have been inclined to set aside Asset Protection Trusts of any type. Accordingly, clients should be aware that the filing of bankruptcy is certain to bring about persistent and successful assaults on many Asset Protection structures. As a result, bankruptcy should be avoided by clients who own assets and have implemented plans to protect them.

Many states have very favorable homestead exemption laws for personal residences. These exemption laws provide a specified—or, in some cases (Florida, Texas), an unlimited—monetary haven for funds invested into a personal residence. The bankruptcy laws require, however, that the debtor must have been domiciled for 730 days prepetition before seeking the state's local exemption laws. Moreover, under the new bankruptcy provisions, a debtor's homestead exemption amount is held at $125,000 if he or she acquired the residence less than 1,215 days prepetition.

Other Exemptions and Protections

Life insurance is also protected and exempt to a varying degree in most states. Annuities are also protected with respect to their cash value, and in a few states even annuity payments are protected.

There is unlimited protection for qualified plans and rollover IRAs under ERISA (the Federal Act that regulates most qualified retirement plans) in a bankruptcy situation. Moreover, there is a $1 million aggregate protection for IRAs. **These exemptions, however, only apply to bankruptcy.** Outside of bankruptcy, if a creditor is seeking to enforce a judgment against a debtor, there is unlimited protection for qualified plans under ERISA—with the caveat that the qualified plan must have other participants beside the sole debtor/business owner. There are broadly drawn state law protections for IRAs that do not come within the blanket coverage of ERISA. For instance, many states allow creditor exemption for IRAs based on the reasonable need of the debtor. The amount of the reasonable need is determined by an economic analysis, taking into account the debtor's age, living standards and cost of living requirements in the area in which the debtor resides.

In June of 2014, the US Supreme Court ruled that funds in an inherited IRA are not protected in bankruptcy (*Clark vs. Rameker*). A popular strategy to protect IRA assets from creditors is to name a Trust rather than a person as the beneficiary of the IRA. Obviously, retirement planning is critical for financial, income tax, estate tax, and Asset Protection planning and should only be undertaken with the assistance of an expert in this area.

Adequate Insurance

There is really no substitute for adequate personal and business insurance; it is always the first line of defense. Individuals should consider maxing out automobile insurance limits and should make sure their homeowners' insurance is sufficient. An umbrella insurance policy is a very good investment because it is reasonably priced and based on one's automobile or homeowner insurance.

In business operations, it is important to obtain expert insurance advice concerning commercial general liability insurance and the amount thereof. Once again, umbrella insurance is strongly recommended. Professionals should obtain as much professional liability insurance as they can reasonably afford. Businesses should consider errors-and-omissions insurance when applicable.

Many business owners and professionals never take the time to read and understand their business insurance policies. A knowledgeable insurance consultant can assist them in understanding their insurance coverage and limits.

TIP

For individuals with substantial assets, it usually makes sense to purchase broad coverage on all fronts: automobile, home, professional liability, and umbrella coverage.

Joint Ownership of Property

Joint ownership of property is generally not a substantial barrier to creditor attacks. Tenancy in common and joint tenancy interests can be reached by creditors. Some states provide for tenancy by the entirety, which cannot be reached by the creditors of only one spouse. But this protection is available in only a handful of states and usually only for real estate. Tenancy by the entirety protection ends when the marriage ends by divorce or death. The typical Revocable Living Trust set up as part of the fundamental Estate Plan affords no protection whatsoever from creditors. Assets in the family Revocable Trust (unless they are placed in a Domestic Asset Protection Trust) can be levied on and seized by creditors.

Marital Planning

In a marriage that is very solid and relatively free of the possibility of divorce, a couple should consider converting some of their jointly held properties to the separate property of the non-working spouse. If possible, the best protection is to transfer the property as a fair market exchange. For example, the non-working spouse can give up an interest in some of his or her property which would be more difficult for creditors to seize, in exchange for the working professional spouse giving up an interest in property that would be easier for creditors to seize. When it comes to marital property planning, however, one has to remember that what is good for the gander is good for the goose: what shields the spouse or couple from Outside Creditors through Asset Protection Planning will probably also shield the assets from spousal claims against the other during divorce proceedings. More-over, agreements between spouses may be subject to avoidance as a fraudulent conveyance. This again emphasizes the necessity of advance planning.

Included here is a hypothetical fact situation to illustrate the concept of Marital Planning for Asset Protection purposes. James is an architect who has been in business for several years providing architectural services for luxury custom homes and remodels. He and his wife, Ava, have been married for several years and have three minor children. Among their assets is their own luxury custom home that James designed and built. James and Ava are fully invested in their marriage, which is solidified by their desire to raise and provide the best environment possible for their three minor children. James and Ava consult an experienced and well-reputed Estate and Asset Protection Planning Attorney. One of the strategies recommended to them is to place their residence solely in Ava's name as her separate property. In consideration for this property, Ava gives up all of her rights to James' architectural practice. In follow-up to this transfer, Ava sets up her own Separate Property Trust into which she places her residence. James' architectural practice is incorporated and has been placed into his own Separate Property Trust. Obviously, depending on the extent of their assets and net worth, other strategies should be implemented. However, if in the future James is sued for architectural malpractice, the couple's residence should be safe and secure in Ava's Separate Property Trust.

CHAPTER

8

Step Four on the Ladder

Liability Protective Entities for Investment Assets

We have previously discussed the importance of establishing and maintaining liability-protected entities for investment assets. In the case of business entities, the corporate form is a traditional form of doing business; corporations provide the necessary shield of liability for operating business assets and are the most common vehicle selected for business operations. Most business operations that produce commodities and own hard assets like equipment utilize the corporate form. Limited Liability Companies (LLC) are more popular for consulting services and internet companies that really act more or less as distributors and have no traditional hard assets such as equipment and fixtures.

When it comes to investment assets, however, the LLC is the entity of choice. LLCs are utilized instead of corporations because they provide more flexibility tax-wise and have the same shield of liability as the corporation. The LLC is a passive entity for tax purposes because it is either a disregarded entity (taxed like a Proprietorship) if it is a single-member LLC, or a pass-through entity (taxed like a Partnership) if it is a multi-member LLC. (Note that the LLC can also elect to be taxed as a Chapter S Corporation or even a C Corporation.)

In talking about liability protection, we have to differentiate between Inside Creditors and Outside Creditors. This concept has been previously discussed in the Introduction contained in Chapter 1 of this book. To review, Inside Creditors are those creditors who have claims against the entity that contains the asset itself. For example, if a business owner or professional has a rental property and places that property within an LLC, and if someone gets hurt at the rental property, the claim can only be directed against the LLC. The owner's personal assets are, therefore, protected from such Inside claims. Inside Debt protection in and of itself is of major importance and should be addressed by placing all real estate assets except for personal residences within LLCs. The LLC is a better vehicle for real estate than an S Corporation because, for tax reasons, indebtedness of the real estate can be allocated to the member owner's tax basis. Moreover, upon the death of a member owner, the member interest may be able to obtain a step-up in tax basis equal to the fair market value at the date of the member's death. These two favorable tax consequences are not available with respect to the S Corporation. Accordingly, all real estate investments should be placed severally in LLCs.

Real Estate Assets

Many business owners and professionals purchase real estate as investments or as vacation homes. These real estate assets expose the owner to tremendous liability. Much of this liability can be covered by insurance. However, there are many claims that are either not within the purview of the insurance coverage or that may exceed the policy limits. In the litigious society we live in, with the deep-pocket theory and victim-oriented philosophy being promulgated in our court system, all real estate investments should be placed within liability-protected entities to protect the owner's other assets from being exposed to liability directed against the owner's real estate assets.

By placing rental-income-producing property and unimproved real estate investments into LLCs, the owner shields his or her other assets from attack stemming from claims against the real estate parcel itself.

> The Limited Liability Company is generally the preferred entity for investment assets and real estate because it provides liability protection and more flexibility on tax issues.

NOTE

Let us review a hypothetical case study that, unfortunately, is all too real in our modern-day, lawsuit-infected society. Ed is a successful real estate broker. He and his wife, Patricia, own several rental properties, including one apartment complex that has 36 units. An explosion occurs at the apartment complex as a result of some propane gas and gasoline stored by one of the apartment tenants. A young child is severely burned as a result of the explosion, and the parents file a multi-million dollar claim for damages against Ed and Patricia. The claim is well in excess of the insurance coverage. Fortunately, however, Ed and Patricia have done some advanced Asset Protection Planning, and the apartment house is contained within a Limited Liability Company they have organized. Although the apartment house itself can be attacked by the victim, their other personal and business assets are protected because of the liability shield that the LLC (which contains the apartment complex) provides.

In another example, however, Dan owns some unimproved property in a recreational area in the mountains a few hours from his residence. Two young boys play on the property, and one falls out of a tree on the property and is paralyzed. Dan has not placed the property in any kind of a liability-protected entity because he did not think there would be any activity on the property that would generate claims. As a result, Dan's house, his business and other assets are subject to the multi-million-dollar claims of the victim. If the property had been placed in an LLC, only the property itself would have been at risk and not Dan's other assets. Clients should be aware of state property tax laws and state LLC specific taxes in evaluating the real estate transfer process.

Segregating Assets into Multiple Liability-Protected Entities

Many businesses have various assets that can be segregated and placed into multiple liability-protected entities. For example, a landscaping company can place all of its equipment and tools into a separate LLC. The LLC can then rent the equipment and tools to the corporation that provides the landscaping services. Many construction companies place their expensive equipment into separate entities so it will be more difficult for creditors of the business to attack them. There may also be some favorable tax consequence and Estate Planning considerations with respect to such an arrangement.

Normally, real estate used in a business should be kept outside of the entity that operates the business, and real estate should never be placed into a C Corporation because of the potential double tax consequences upon its sale. Doctors and other professionals who own the buildings in which they practice should have the buildings placed into LLCs and then leased to the entity that operates their practice or renders the professional services.

TIP

Segregating various business assets into separate LLCs affords a large measure of protection against creditors.

The foregoing principle is aptly demonstrated by the Richard and Becky Fact Situation we referred to in Chapter 1. They have a corporation that operates a small distribution business. The office and warehouse is headquartered in a small commercial building that has been placed in an LLC by Richard and Becky. The LLC then leases the building to the distribution corporation.

Another good example of the foregoing is the hypothetical case of Glenn, who operates an automobile dealership. The property upon which the dealership operates is placed into a separate LLC and is leased to the corporation that operates the dealership. All of the service equipment and tools are in yet another LLC and leased to the dealership corporation. By segregating these assets into different liability-protected entities, Glenn has set up a structure that will be more difficult for creditors to attack. Glenn may also grant an interest to his children in these LLCs that own property and equipment, and this procedure can prove to be an effective Estate Planning tool, as well.

The Charging Order and Protection against Outside Debts

As advantageous as the tax factors of an LLC and Partnership are, one of the primary benefits of a Limited Partnership or an LLC is that the creditors of the debtor partner or member are, for the most part, limited to the remedy of a Charging Order. A Charging Order is more or less an assignment of income ordered by the Court in favor of the creditor, requiring that any future distributions from the Limited Partnership or LLC to the debtor (whether limited partner or member) be made to the creditor who obtained the Charging Order. The beneficiary of the Charging Order does not become a partner or member and theoretically obtains no voting rights. The General Partner or Manager of the Limited Partnership and LLC, respectively, can therefore retain control over any distributions. By obtaining a Charging Order, the creditor may put itself in the position of being responsible for income taxes on Partnership or LLC income even though no distributions are made. Accordingly, the creditor is faced with additional and substantial financial risk in obtaining a Charging Order. This risk, combined with the delaying nature of the Charging Order, acts as a substantial deterrent to creditor action, or at the very least, gives the debtor much more leverage with which to deal with the creditor when it comes to settlement negotiations.

What Is a Charging Order?

A Charging Order is a court mandate available to a judgment creditor directed to the Partnership or LLC (of which the judgment debtor is a partner or member), which grants the judgment creditor the right to whatever distributions would otherwise be due to the debtor partner or member whose interest is being charged. This remedy is only available to a judgment creditor, which means a creditor must first successfully sue the debtor and obtain a judgment for a specific sum of money. Specifically, the debtor's Partnership or LLC interest—not the debtor or the LLC/Partnership itself—would be charged to satisfy the judgment. This is an important distinction to make in order to understand the limitations of a Charging Order and the issues involved with the foreclosure of a Charging Order, and is discussed below. A Charging Order is a remedy that is only available to "Outside Creditors" for the satisfaction of Outside Debts (as explained earlier). In other words, it is a remedy only available to a creditor who has obtained a personal judgment against the LP partner or member of the LLC.

Historical Background of the Charging Order

The Charging Order originated as a part of the English Partnership Act of 1890. The relevant provisions of that Act are very close to similar provisions later adopted in the United States in the Uniform Partnership Act in 1914 and the Uniform Limited Partnership Act in 1916. The purpose of the Charging Order was to prevent the judgment creditor of an individual partner from gaining access to the Partnership assets, while at the same time giving the creditor some recourse via distributions from the entity to

> A Charging Order is a court mandate that gives the creditor income or distributions from the Partnership that would otherwise accrue to the benefit of the debtor.

NOTE

the partner. The Charging Order then became the exclusive remedy of the judgment creditor of a partner denying the creditor direct access to the Partnership assets. It limits the creditor exclusively to the collection of the income or distributions that the Partnership assets might otherwise produce for the benefit of the judgment debtor.

An ownership or equity interest in an entity consists of a bundle of rights and obligations that can be segregated. These rights and obligations are set by default under the applicable statute. Many of these "default" rights and duties may be altered by agreement of the partners. Examples of some of these rights and duties include economic rights, e.g., the right to receive distributions of money or other capital from the business entity, management rights, voting rights and the obligation to make additional capital contributions.

A Charging Order is a relatively limited remedy that only gives the creditor the right to receive distributions—if and when the person or persons with the authority to determine the distributions choose to do so. For example, in an LLC, the Manager usually has the exclusive right to determine if and when distributions will be made to the members. However, the Manager is always, at least in properly structured Asset Protection Plans, either the debtor himself or someone friendly to the debtor. Thus, the Manager may determine to continually reinvest the profits back into the business, leaving nothing or little for distributions to the members, or, in this case, the creditor. However, this situation favors the party best suited to wait out the settlement. If the debtor and other members of the LLC rely on distributions more than the creditor needs the proceeds, the members may have little choice but to settle with the creditor. The distribution scheme of a charging order is displayed in Figure 8.1.

Because the Charging Order only gives the creditor the right to receive the debtor's *pro-rata* share of any distributions, the debtor retains any and all management, voting and other rights associated with the charged LLC interest. The fact remains, however, that the Charging Order remedy substantially limits the creditor and gives the debtor member or partner great leverage in working out a settlement and, at times, denying the creditor any worthwhile release at all.

In many states, the Charging Order remedy is not the exclusive remedy provided by statute or case law. Accordingly, aggressive creditors may petition the court for Charging Order provisions that control management activities and which may ultimately be able to access the assets within the LLC itself.

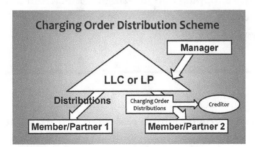

Figure 8.1. Charging Order Distribution Scheme

In order to better understand the effect of the Charging Order, let us examine a hypothetical situation: a creditor has obtained a personal judgment against Brian, who owns and operates a small business operation in a corporation. The creditor can examine Brian and find out what his assets are and where they are located. If the corporation has any value, the creditor can attach Brian's corporate stock, which represents his ownership in the corporation. The creditor can then, through either a private or a public auction, bid on a portion or all of the judgment against Brian and become the owner of the corporation. The judgment creditor (as the shareholder) can then appoint himself or herself as a director and president of the Company and can liquidate its assets in order to satisfy the judgment.

> **NOTE**
>
> Charging Order remedies vary from state to state, with some states providing creditors an access path to management activities and the assets of the entity. Check with your attorney.

Contrast the foregoing with this situation: Brian's business is owned in an LLC instead of the corporation, and the LLC is located in a state which provides that the Charging Order is the exclusive remedy for a creditor. In this instance, all the creditor can do is to obtain an attachment or a lien on any distributions made by the business to Brian. The creditor cannot reach the assets within the LLC and is only entitled to any amount of distributions that are made.

From the foregoing examples, it is easy to see that a Charging Order affords Brian much more protection, as otherwise, a creditor could attack the assets of the business directly.

Forum Shopping

Because some states have better Charging Order protection laws than others, many attorneys recommend utilizing these favorable state LLCs rather than the LLC of domicile. For example, a California business owner may want to consider utilizing a Delaware, Nevada, Wyoming, or Arizona LLC instead of a California LLC because these states have legislation that provides that the Charging Order is the exclusive remedy.

There is no guarantee that the California courts would honor the exclusive remedy provisions of the out-of-state LLC, but at least it gives the business owner an issue that has to be litigated, and provides a substantial barrier to the creditor. Accordingly, by forum shopping and utilizing an LLC from a more favorable jurisdiction, the business owner or professional gives himself or herself more leverage in dealing with a creditor.

The Series LLC

Many corporations and LLCs own and operate more than one business, and many individual investors own multiple real estate properties titled under a single name or business entity. The problem with single ownership of multiple businesses or properties is that any legal claim asserted against one business or asset jeopardizes all the other assets or businesses. Therefore, many businesses and investors with multiple businesses or properties segregate the ownership of such businesses or properties so that a claim against one business or property will not taint the owner's other assets. This process of liability segregation can become expensive and complicated as new and different entities are set up and maintained for each separate business or property.

While a Series LLC may sound attractive on the surface, they can be complex to execute, give rise to difficult tax issues and uncertainty over cross-state enforcement.

Delaware, Nevada and certain other states have addressed this issue by creating a new type of legal entity which permits intra-entity shields based on a series classification. The Series LLC provides for one master LLC to establish several different series or sub-LLCs under the same general LLC umbrella, as shown in Figure 8.2. Each separate series or sub-LLC is able to own distinct assets, incur separate liabilities and have different managers and members. The master LLC pays only one filing fee and may file only one income tax return each year. If separate records are maintained, the assets for any one series are accounted for separately from the assets of the other series, and through a notice of the limitation of liability set forth in the Articles of Organization of the master LLC, the debtor obligations of that series may not be enforced against the rest of the entity or the other series.

Uses

One of the most important applications of the Series LLC is the ownership of multiple parcels of real property. It is, obviously, less expensive than creating, filing and maintaining several different LLCs to segregate property ownership. Another possible benefit might be the transfer of assets among related businesses without income tax, or built in gain or liability for real estate transfer taxes.

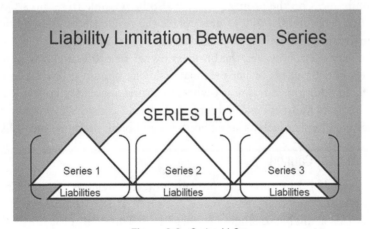

Figure 8.2. Series LLCs

Experience has shown that there are several problems with respect to structuring the Series LLC. The master Operating Agreement for a Series LLC provides for the creation of more than one series. Each series can have different members, managers, assets, and liabilities. The members and managers of each series may have different rights, duties, and authority. As a result of this, the Operating Agreement and the specific addendums for each particular series are difficult to draft and can be somewhat confusing. Moreover, the series structure will undoubtedly be very confusing for financial institutions and title companies as the individual requires their services. With respect to the income tax consequences, because there is a lack of clear federal tax standards for Series LLCs with multiple members, it may be difficult to determine the best method for tax reporting. Should the Series LLC only have one Federal Employer Identification Number (FEIN) and file one general return or should each series have a separate FEIN and file a separate return? The answer may get complicated.

Another problem with the Series LLC is that the state of domicile that does not have Series LLC legislation may not recognize the distinct series features of the non-domicile Series LLC's state. For example, California may not recognize the separate liability provisions of the Nevada or Delaware Series LLC laws. Therefore, a California resident may hesitate to utilize a Nevada or Delaware Series LLC because of the uncertainty of whether or not the California courts will enforce the other state's series legislation. Accordingly, many residents of states without series legislation are reluctant to utilize the series structure because of the uncertainty regarding the enforcement of the series provisions within the domiciliary state.

Conclusion

In conclusion, we have discussed the importance for all real estate assets other than personal residences to be placed in LLCs. A personal residence cannot be placed into an LLC because there is no business purpose for doing so. In order to create a business purpose, the owner of the personal residence would have to pay rent to the LLC, which does not really make much sense. The best protection for a personal residence is to "equity strip it" by obtaining loans and placing mortgage encumbrances on the property. It may also be possible to set up a Qualified Personal Residence Trust (QPRT) or to place the residence in a Domestic Asset Protection Trust, which will be discussed in the next chapter.

At the very least, however, the business owner or professional who has real estate assets outside of his or her personal residence should utilize LLCs to own such assets. In addition, if business owners or professionals are concerned about Outside Creditors and personal liability, they should consider placing even their other investment assets such as stock holdings and bank accounts into LLCs.

One Final Word of Caution

The single-member LLC provides needed protection against Inside Creditors. However, recent court cases have made it clear that the Charging Order remedy may not be available to single-member LLCs. The reason for this is that the

Charging Order remedy is designed to protect other members or partners. If there are no other members or partners in an LLC, there does not seem to be any reason for maintaining Charging Order protection. Accordingly, for maximum Outside Creditor protection (personal liability), the LLCs should be created as multi-member LLCs. Children, other relatives or close friends can be utilized as minority members of the LLC. It should be noted that Nevada, Wyoming, Delaware and South Dakota all have specific legislation making the Charging Order the exclusive creditor remedy against single-member (as well as multimember) LLCs. However, other states may not choose to follow such legislation.

Step Five on the Ladder

Domestic Asset Protection Trusts and Modular Planning Utilizing LLCs

As discussed in Chapter 6, there are many advantages in creating and utilizing Domestic Trusts.

- Probate is avoided, which eliminates the cost and inconvenience associated with the Probate court structure.
- The transfer of assets is more efficient because it can be accomplished during the lifetime of the Trust makers (or Trustors) who have more knowledge about their property and assets than their heirs would have.
- Confidentiality is maintained because no court procedures (namely Probate), which are a matter of public record, are required.

However, the typical family Living Trust affords no Asset Protection whatsoever for the Trustor. The Trust can include spendthrift provisions that will protect a third-party beneficiary's interest in the Trust from creditor's claims, but these spendthrift provisions do not protect the Trustor. Nevertheless, they can be effective for protecting beneficiaries against creditor claims.

For well over a hundred years, individuals in the US and elsewhere have utilized foreign Self-Settled Trusts to protect their assets. Many offshore jurisdictions have either Trust-enabling legislation or favorable court decisions that provide creditor protection for Self-Settled Trusts. Because of this protection, several offshore jurisdictions have a very substantial Trust industry servicing foreign Asset Protection Trusts.

Recently, several US states have adopted legislation similar to various off-shore jurisdictions. These statutory provisions provide various degrees of Asset Protection for a Settlor's interest as a beneficiary in a Self-Settled Trust.

Setting Up and Maintaining Domestic Asset Protection Trusts

Fourteen states now have legislation providing for Settlor protection to a Settlor/beneficiary of an Asset Protection Trust:

- Alaska
- Nevada
- Missouri
- Utah
- Wyoming
- New Hampshire
- Colorado
- Delaware
- South Dakota
- Rhode Island
- Tennessee
- Oklahoma
- Hawaii
- Ohio

As of this printing, other states are considering adopting similar legislation. This phenomenon of Domestic Asset Protection Trust (DAPT) legislation indicates a strong trend in the US in favor of providing Asset Protection for individuals setting up Self-Settled Trusts.

For maximum Asset Protection, there are several attributes that the Asset Protection Trust must have. First, it has to be created in the state that has the enabling legislation. The four states that have the best statutory structure, in my opinion, are Alaska, Delaware, Nevada and South Dakota.

For maximum Asset Protection purposes, the following features should be included in each Domestic Asset Protection Trust:

Asset Protection Trusts offered by a number of states mirror the structures and provisions of foreign Trusts that have grown enormously popular over many decades.

NOTE

- The Trust should have an independent Trustee in residence in the state with the favorable Trust legislation in order to create the Trust within that region.
- The Trustee should be given sole discretion for income or principal distributions.
- The Trustee should be given power to make payments on the beneficiaries' behalf rather than directly to them.
- The Trustee should be authorized to request assets for use of beneficiaries.
- The Trustee should be given the power to hold back distributions.
- Any power of appointment by a beneficiary should be limited.
- The Trustee can be given additional sprinkling powers with respect to distributions among a class of beneficiaries.
- A spendthrift provision should be included. This provision gives the Trustee discretionary powers with respect to the making of distributions.

- Each asset or groups of assets should be owned by the Trust in liability-shielded entities, so that any claim against one asset cannot be inserted against another asset.

Consequences of Utilizing Domestic Asset Protection Trusts

If properly set up and maintained, the DAPT will be a significant barrier to creditors and will afford significant leverage to the debtor's negotiations with the creditor. This is especially true if the assets of the Trust that need to be protected are located in a state that is the domiciliary of the DAPT. The main problem with the utilization of a DAPT is that the courts of the nondomiciliary state may not recognize the Asset Protection features of the Trust. However, there is no question that a significant degree of protection is afforded by utilizing the DAPT—especially when it comes to negotiating for a settlement with the creditor. As stated above, it is strongly recommended that a professional Trustee be utilized with a DAPT; in fact, such a Trustee may be mandatory in many instances. The attack of creditors in a non-Asset Protection Trust state against the DAPT will be more successful if the DAPT is a self-settled Trust—in other words, if the maker of the Trust is also the beneficiary of the Trust. This, of course, can be a major problem if the client does not want to make the transfers to the Trust completed gifts and wants to be able to retain enough control over the assets of the DAPT, so that the client can ultimately be the beneficiary of the assets. A non-self-settled DAPT which most likely requires that it be a completed gift transfer is more likely to withstand a contested creditor proceeding in a non-DAPT state.

TIP — By creatively structuring a Domestic Asset Protection Trust with a Limited Liability entity, the effectiveness of a Charging Order judgment on the Asset Protection structure can be substantially reduced.

A leading case in this area was an Alaska Bankruptcy Case in 2011 referred to as the *Mortensen Case*. Mortensen was an Alaska resident who set up an Alaska Asset Protection Trust and funded it with Alaska real property in 2005. After creating the Trust, Mortensen accrued over $250,000 in credit card debt. He filed for bankruptcy in 2009 after major health problems and the loss of his job. The Bankruptcy Court voided the transfer of property to the Trust and ruled that the property was an asset of the Bankruptcy Estate. Although Mortensen did some things right, his biggest mistake was filing for bankruptcy after the State's statute of limitations had already run. Moreover, as was stated previously, DAPTs are not likely to stand up in bankruptcy if they are self-settled. Mortensen was not an ideal Asset Protection client because he had a very small net worth. He admitted that his transfer into the DAPT was for Asset Protection planning purposes. He was on the verge of running up significant debts and he tried to accomplish all his planning without legal counsel.

In spite of Mortensen and other cases, DAPTs can work. They are certainly not bullet proof, but they do provide a significant firewall of protection against creditor claims. They may have a better chance of working if they are non self-settled or completed gift Trusts, but not all clients can set up the DAPT in a completed gift structure.

When setting up a DAPT, the fraudulent transfer law must be carefully analyzed because the creditor will be able to set aside the transfer to the Trust if it is deemed to be a fraudulent conveyance. Although the timing of the transfer with respect to the creditor claim plays a key role in triggering a fraudulent conveyance claim, most of the DAPT provisions of the various states with enabling legislation also provide statutes of limitations for challenging transfers to the Trust. Nevada has the most favorable statute in this regard. It provides that a creditor may only bring action against the Trust (1) within two years after the transfer to the Trust or (2) six months after the creditor discovers or reasonably should have discovered the transfer, whichever is later. If someone becomes a creditor after the transfer to the Trust is made, any action in Nevada must be brought within two years after the transfer.

Modular Structuring Utilizing DAPT and LLCs

One of the best Asset Protection strategies is to combine the utilization of the DAPT with an LLC. In this circumstance, the member interest of the owner of the LLC is transferred to the DAPT, which holds the interest more or less as a custodian. For example, a husband or wife can be a Trustor, or the maker of a DAPT. An LLC can then be set up to hold real property, and the member interest can be transferred to the DAPT. Another LLC can be set up to hold liquid investments, and (again) the member interest can be transferred to the DAPT. It is recommended that a third party own at least 5% of the LLC because, as mentioned previously, the efficacy of the Charging Order is greatly reduced and even eliminated when the LLC is a single-member LLC. A diagram of the structure is shown in Figure 9.1.

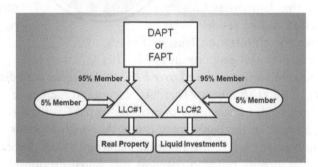

Figure 9.1. The Modular Structuring Diagram

Divided You Stand; United You Fall

If an individual owns everything in one company or in his or her own name, one lawsuit can result in that individual losing everything he or she owns. However, if assets are spread around in the different liability-protected entities, then only the entity involved in the suit may be at risk. What this means is that most valuable assets should be segregated into separate LLCs, as we have previously discussed.

In order to better understand the utilization of the DAPT, let us examine a few hypothetical case studies.

Hypothetical Case Study No. 1

For example, Derrick Sanders and his wife, Melanie, own two income-producing real properties and several percentage investments in other real estate projects. Derrick is a building contractor and developer and is not only worried about liability for his real estate and business interests, but also has concerns about personal liability with respect to loans he has guaranteed and other potential building-related claims. He and Melanie set up a DAPT and place their income-producing properties in separate LLCs and some other investments and liquidities in other LLCs. Derrick's sister, Janice, is given a small interest in some of the other LLCs. If creditors try to assert personal liability against Derrick and are successful in obtaining a judgment, they will have to try to enforce the judgment by going against the DAPT, as well as the various LLCs where they may be limited only to a Charging Order remedy. The example is diagramed in Figure 9.2.

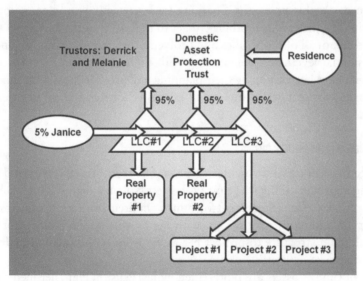

Figure 9.2. Derrick and Melanie Case Study

Hypothetical Case Study No. 2

Jim Collins and Steve Bresnic are the co-founders and 50% owners of a small, but highly successful electrical circuit and semi-conductor manufacturing company (C&B Circuits). They have recently sold the Company for an amount in excess of $40 million, the proceeds of which represent much of their respective estates, except for their respective personal residences, a commercial building they jointly own, a few residential rental properties they jointly own and an airplane they jointly own and pilot.

Obviously, Jim and Steve have potential liability problems. The buyer of the business could come back against them for allegations of misrepresentation in the sale of the business. They also have potential liability with respect to the commercial building and the rental properties they jointly own. And, of course, the airplane is a great risk and has major, major liability potential. Separate LLCs should be set up for the commercial building and the residential rental properties. The airplane should also be placed into an LLC. Jim and his spouse and Steve and his spouse should consider setting up DAPTs and utilizing them in the modular structure explained previously. The LLC interests owned by Jim and Steve can be transferred to their respective DAPTs. Jim and Steve can each continue to manage the LLCs, and in the event any major liability is asserted against either of them, they can resign as managers and appoint a favorable third party to manage the LLCs. In the event of a lawsuit against either or both Jim and Steve, the creditor will have to first obtain a judgment against them. Then, in order to enforce the judgment, the creditor will have to sue the Trustee of the DAPT and try to attack the legal viability of the Trust structure. This can be very expensive and time-consuming. The lawsuit may have to be initiated in the state in which the Trustee is domiciled. Even if the creditor is successful in obtaining a judgment against the Trustee, the creditor will then have to go against the LLCs in order to enforce the judgment. At this point, the Charging Order remedy would come into play, severely limiting the creditor's ability to get to the assets of the LLCs.

As a result of all of the hurdles and problems the creditor faces, Jim and Steve have substantial leverage in negotiating with the creditor for a settlement. The barriers that have been set up by their planning will provide them with substantial protection and make it very difficult and expensive for the creditor to enforce any judgment.

Hypothetical Case Study No. 3

Cindy Reed is a practicing vascular surgeon. She is in her early 40s and is contemplating marriage for the first time with Brett Nolan, a high school teacher and Boys Basketball Coach. Brett has two minor children from a previous marriage and a very acrimonious relationship with his ex-wife. Cindy wants not only a prenuptial, but a structure to protect her assets from both potential malpractice claims and attacks by Brett's ex-wife.

Most of Cindy's assets are represented by her Pension Plan, her medical practice, her personal residence, and a Palm Desert Condo. Cindy and her brother, who is also a physician, will also inherit substantial assets from their widowed mother.

Again, a DAPT is definitely an option Cindy should strongly consider. The Trust will enhance the protection of her prenuptial agreement, but also set up an important structure to protect her assets from both potential malpractice claims and attacks by Brett's ex-wife. She can set up a DAPT and convey her personal residence directly into the Trust. She should consider stripping much of the equity out of the residence and placing the proceeds, plus other investments that can be contributed, to an LLC. Her Palm Desert condo should also be placed into an LLC. The LLC member interest should be placed into Cindy's DAPT. Cindy's pension plan, if properly structured, will be protected from creditor attack. Cindy and her brother should also consult a qualified Estate and Asset Protection Planning attorney with respect to the substantial assets they will inherit from their widowed mother. An Inheritance DAPT can be established as the receptacle for the property they will inherit from their mother.

The foregoing case studies illustrate the importance of proper planning and the utilization of LLCs in conjunction with DAPTs. The Modular Structure involved (as illustrated in Figures 5 and 6 above) provide strong firewalls of protection. The LLC itself is one firewall, and another strong firewall is constructed by transferring the LLC interest to a DAPT.

The Trust Protector

Many offshore Trusts commonly use a Trust Protector to protect the interests of the Trustor and the beneficiaries of the Trust. Trust Protectors are also now utilized with DAPTs. The Protector is a third party to whom the Trustor gives discretion over certain functions:

- The power to amend the Trust
- The power to change Trust situs (or domicile) to another jurisdiction when events causing duress occur
- The power to remove the Trustee or to substitute a new Trustee and a new situs jurisdiction
- The power to veto Trustee decisions
- The power to veto distributions

The Protector can be a relative, friend, or a third-party professional. Ideally, the Protector should be someone outside of the jurisdiction of the Trust maker. The utilization of a Trust Protector affords the maker of the Trust much greater flexibility and more current Trust planning than the Trust maker would have without the utilization of a Protector.

The DAPT is particularly effective when it is combined with the utilization of LLCs. The professional or business executive and his or her family are the beneficiaries of the DAPT, but don't technically own the assets within the Trust. Thus, this rung of the ladder provides a substantial firewall as protection against creditors.

Step Six on the Ladder

The Offshore Asset Protection Trust and the Modular Planning that Accompanies It

For well over a 100 years, US citizens and many foreigners have utilized Offshore Trusts for Asset Protection Planning purposes. Often, when individuals hear mention of offshore structures, they think of a scheming design to evade taxation reporting. Legitimate offshore planning, however, has nothing to do with tax evasion. Tax evasion is a felony in the United States and is not and should not be the objective of any good citizen/reasonable person. The consequences of a felony conviction—including jail time—should deter anyone from considering tax evasion. Offshore tax dodges have given offshore planning a bad name, but there is nothing wrong with setting up an offshore structure for Asset Protection Planning purposes. Such structures are usually tax neutral, but do require substantial reporting and compliance with IRS forms and regulations. Filing these documents, however, is not a huge burden if one has the proper CPA and legal advisors.

Basically, there are three factors that should be present when going offshore for Asset Protection Planning purposes. First, the individual involved should have substantial liquid assets that can be placed offshore. The goal is to set up a nest egg and protect these assets. The whole reason for going offshore is to place assets outside of the jurisdiction of the United States; offshore planning requires there be enough liquid assets to transfer offshore, so as to make the structure worthwhile. A second factor in deciding whether to go offshore (which is not a determining requirement, but does help to sustain the offshore structure) is international connections. For example, if the US resident has relatives or family offshore, then the offshore structure makes more sense. Also, if the US resident owns property offshore or does business

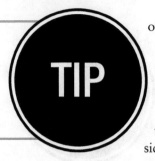

Who should consider an off-shore Asset Protection Trust? Anyone with substantial assets who requires a large degree of protection.

offshore, then the offshore structure becomes more viable.

The final factor is the degree of protection the individual requires. Because the offshore structure is much more protected, individuals who need the most protection should always consider going offshore.

Setting Up and Maintaining the Foreign Asset Protection Trust

A Foreign Asset Protection Trust (FAPT) is a Trust that is set up in an offshore jurisdiction that has enabling Trust legislation providing for substantial protection against creditors of the Trustor. One of the greatest advantages of an FAPT is the fact that, by its very nature, any legal attack against the assets is transferred abroad to a different legal system. A foreign Trustee is necessary for the efficacy of the FAPT. As stated, the biggest advantage in utilizing the FAPT is that assets can be placed offshore beyond the jurisdiction of the US courts.

Some of the advantages of FAPT are as follows:

- Most foreign jurisdictions do not recognize US judgments. This may force a new trial on the merits in the foreign situs country.
- Some foreign situs jurisdictions require a much more difficult burden of proof for a creditor to challenge asset transfers to the foreign Asset Protection Trust.
- Some jurisdictions have a statute of limitations for challenging asset transfers to a FAPT that begins to run on the date of transfer.
- Fees and expenses in litigating in foreign jurisdictions are substantial, thereby serving as a strong deterrent to foreign litigation.
- The FAPT minimizes the likelihood of a fraudulent conveyance charge because of the difficulty to a creditor of proceeding against the transferee Trustee located in the foreign jurisdiction.
- The FAPT prevents attachment against assets placed in the offshore structure outside of US jurisdiction.
- The foreign structure makes any type of an injunction against further disposition of assets extremely unlikely.
- The FAPT practically eliminates the possibility of the appointment of a receiver over the transferred assets.
- The foreign structure places the assets in a jurisdiction whose laws are favorable to debtors and hostile to creditors.
- An Offshore Trust with at least one US beneficiary is a Grantor Trust for tax purposes. As a result, the FAPT is a pass-through entity to the Grantor, similar to a Revocable Trust when it comes to tax reporting.
- Transfers to FAPT are normally incomplete gifts. Accordingly, the assets are generally included in the Grantor's estate for estate tax purposes.

- Most FAPTs provide for the office of a Trust Protector. The third-party Protector has the power to remove the Trustee and appoint a substitute Trustee to change the situs of the Trust. He or she can also veto any amendments or distributions made by the Trust. Many times, the Protector can be an entity or person not subject to the jurisdiction of a US court.
- Anti-duress provisions make it very difficult for any court order to have any impact on Trustee or creditor attacks designed to force distributions from the Trust to the creditor.

To recapitulate, the FAPT places assets out-of-reach of US courts. Creditors are required to litigate in offshore jurisdictions, utilizing offshore domicile laws and justice systems rather than the US court process.

Factors and Jurisdiction-Selection Process

There are many factors involved in selecting the proper jurisdiction for an Offshore Trust. First and foremost, the foreign situs must have favorable Trust legislation. Secondly, there must be stable and professional Trustees available to serve in that capacity.

Another factor is that the offshore jurisdiction must have favorable tax laws, to ensure that the Trust is not taxed in such jurisdiction.

Another factor is whether the English language predominates in that country, to ensure that there are no language barriers. The domicile should have a stable political situation and modern telecommunication facilities. It should also have a good reputation in the global financial community.

NOTE

The purpose of a Foreign Asset Protection Trust is to protect the assets from US courts. In selecting a jurisdiction, consider Trust legislation, taxes, the judicial system, and the overall financial and political stability.

There should be a provision in the Trust legislation providing for non-recognition of foreign judgments. Hopefully, a criminal burden of proof should be applicable in civil cases. In the United States, the civil burden of proof is a preponderance of the evidence, which means that the court or jury has to be convinced that at least 51% of the evidence favors the plaintiff. In a criminal proceeding in the US, however, the decision must be 100% in favor of the prosecution in order to convict a criminal defendant. In some offshore jurisdictions, the civil burden of proof is 100 to nothing, or beyond a reasonable doubt, as in US criminal cases. Because of the difficult burden of proof, it is very, very difficult for a creditor to obtain a favorable judgment in the offshore jurisdiction.

Finally, the foreign jurisdiction should have a sound judicial system with requirements for litigation by local counsel only and a disallowance of contingency fees. The choice of law clause in the FAPT should generally be upheld, as the parties appoint a Foreign Trustee.

As was stated, Protectors act as watch dogs over Trustees. They have veto powers on the right to terminate the Trustee. The Trustor or the individual setting up the Trust structure should not be made the Protector. The best alternative is to have the Protector be an offshore person or entity outside of the jurisdiction of US courts.

Tax Considerations

Offshore Trusts are deemed a Foreign Trust unless two requirements are met: (1) the US courts must be able to exercise primary supervision over the administration of the Trust; and (2) one or more US persons must have the authority to control all substantial decisions regarding the Trust. For the best Asset Protection consequences, most foreign Asset Protection Trusts will be considered Foreign Trusts for tax purposes.

Even if the Trust is classified as a Foreign Trust, it will be treated as a Grantor Trust under Internal Revenue Code Section 679. This label is applied if the Settlor or Trustor is a US person, if the Trust has US beneficiaries, and the maker of the Trust retains certain Grantor Trust rights as set forth in Sections 671–677 of the Internal Revenue Code. These rights include a retained power of appointment and the power to substitute Trust property.

For the most part, transfers to the Trust are treated as incomplete gifts because there is a retained power of appointment. These incomplete gifts result in the assets of the Trust being included in the Trustor's estate upon death. The Offshore Trust, however, can contain Credit Shelter or By-Pass Trust language, as was explained more specifically in Chapter 6. For income tax purposes, a step-up in the tax basis of a Trust asset (resulting in a forgiveness of capital gain on the death of the Settlor/Trustor) will be preserved if the Trust is included in the estate.

The Cook Islands: The Best Offshore Jurisdiction

Many attorneys and other advisors recommend that individuals who set up offshore structures select the Cook Islands for the situs of the Trust. The Cook Islands are an independent country with a Westminster style Parliament. The Islands gained their independence from New Zealand in 1964. They have a highly educated English speaking labor force and the highest GDP per capita amongst the South Pacific small island nations. They also have a very well-respected judiciary with judges from New Zealand's higher court. There are many competent professionals who provide backup services to the offshore financial services industry and many experienced Trust companies with extremely competent Trust officers.

In the 1980s, the Cook Islands codified the concept of Asset Protection Trust through the enactment of the International Trust Act. The Act modifies certain common law Trust principles that were contrary to Asset Protection. As a result, the Cook Islands are now considered the leading Asset Protection jurisdiction in the world. Its legislation has been copied by other jurisdictions, and it has a long track record in case law that has provided certainty with respect to the Asset Protection features of the Trust.

In the Cook Islands, privacy is guaranteed. Moreover, the requirement of litigating and utilizing the Cook Islands' legal system is a strong deterrent to creditors:

- Creditors must provide a bond for cost.
- Contingency fees are not permitted.
- It is difficult to find a Cook Islands lawyer that has not already been conflicted by the Trustees.

Trust companies are highly regulated in the Cook Islands. They are subject to strict monetary supervision. Professional indemnity insurance is a prerequisite for licensing. There is no local tax on the assets and income of Cook Islands offshore vehicles.

The Cook Islands International Trust Act provides for the following key factors:

- Foreign judgments are not enforceable.
- Self-Settled Trusts are permitted.
- The maker of the Trust is permitted to retain Trust powers and benefits.
- The spendthrift provisions provide that an interest in Trust property cannot be alienated or passed by the bankruptcy of beneficiaries or process of law relating to them.
- The Cook Islands Trust is not void or voidable in the event of the Settlor's bankruptcy.
- The Trust can only be challenged on the grounds of a fraudulent transfer.
- There is a comprehensive fraudulent transfer process, and limited time to commence action against the Trust for fraudulent conveyance. The fraudulent transfer rules are governed by a two-step test:
  - Did the transfer occur within two years of a cause of action arising?
  - If so, did the proceeds commence in the Cook Islands within one year of the settlement or transfer to the Trust?
- The creditor must prove beyond a reasonable doubt that the transfer was made with the principal intent to defraud a specific creditor and that it rendered the Settlor unable to pay that creditor.
- Offshore, fraudulent intent cannot be successfully asserted—even under circumstances in which such intent would almost certainly be found under US fraudulent transfer and conveyance laws.

Issues of Contempt of the Foreign Asset Protection Trusts

The very nature of a creditor attack on an FAPT engenders issues dealing with contempt law with respect to the repatriation of Trust assets. Civil contempt is the means by which a court coerces an individual or entity to comply with a court order. In order to be held in contempt, the individual being charged must generally have the present ability to comply with the court order. If this impossibility of performance is self-created, however, the contempt order may still issue. Contempt problems usually arise in the FAPT context with respect to issues relating to the Trust Protector and the antiduress provisions. Two recent cases, *The Anderson Case* and *The Lawrence Case*, have given rise to much discussion and notoriety. The circumstances of both should be carefully considered with respect to the establishment of FAPTs.

The Anderson Case

Michael and Denyse Anderson were sued by the Federal Trade Commission (FTC) relative to a telemarketing program that was labeled by the court as "A classic Ponzi scheme." The compensation they had appropriated for themselves with respect to the telemarketing ventures was placed overseas in a Cook Islands Trust that had been set up over two years before their involvement in the telemarketing program. During the course of the FTC litigation, the Andersons were ordered to produce certain financial information and to repatriate funds held in the FAPT, which they declined to do. The lower court held the Andersons in contempt and jailed them in Las Vegas, Nevada; and the Appellate court affirmed the lower court's ruling—finding that the Andersons remained in control of the FAPT and could, therefore, comply with the repatriation order. The Andersons had remained co-Trustees of the FAPT throughout the litigation, and it was later discovered by the court that they were also the Protectors of the Trust. Both these facts should not have occurred in a properly structured FAPT.

As with other Asset Protection vehicles, a Foreign Asset Protection Trust will not protect the assets in a situation which will likely lead to a substantial claim against the Trustor.

CAUTION

It is interesting to note that in *The Anderson Case*, the FTC was attempting to seize almost $6 million from the Andersons. The Cook Islands Trustee of their Trust had refused to turn over the assets of the Trust in spite of repeated attempts by the FTC. This case emphasizes how strong the Cook Islands Trustees will be in resisting creditor's attempts to repatriate assets. Ultimately, the FTC settled the case for $1.2 million, and the Andersons were released from jail.

The Lawrence Case

In *The Lawrence Case*, a bankruptcy debtor's complete lack of credibility and blatant lying resulted in him (Lawrence) being incarcerated on contempt charges. Lawrence had established and funded an offshore Asset Protection Trust in the Channel Islands a few weeks before a $20 million binding arbitration award was entered against him. He shortly thereafter transferred the Trust situs to Mauritius.

In Lawrence, the Court went out of its way to point out how the record was replete with inconsistent and vague testimony and outright lies by Lawrence. The following factors, no doubt, heavily influenced the Court in its contempt holding:

- The executed Trust documents were never provided to the Court.
- Lawrence incredulously testified that he was not aware of any distributions to him from the Trust when the evidence showed otherwise.
- Lawrence denied that shielding his assets from his creditors was a motivating factor in the set-up of the FAPT.
- Lawrence testified that the arbitration proceeding did not influence him in any manner in setting up the FAPT.

The record was replete with other inconsistencies and untruths. Suffice it to say that the establishment of a FAPT should not be utilized to shield assets where there are existing facts which give rise to a substantial claim against the potential Trustor. The efficacy of a FAPT is based on long-range planning, and the FAPT should be set up and established to protect the Trustor's assets from unknown and reasonably unforeseen creditors. In this regard, the non-asset-protection aspects of the FAPT should be emphasized (e.g., traditional Estate Planning considerations, including the orderly transfer of wealth between generation, the avoidance of Probate, economic diversification, etc.). It should be noted, however, that there is nothing inherently wrong with the desire to protect one's assets against the claims of future potential creditors—a principle that has been long recognized in the United States with respect to the establishment of corporations, limited partnerships and, more recently, limited liability companies.

After Lawrence spent six years in jail without the court being successful in repatriating the funds, he was released in 2006. The District Court Judge stated that "apparently imprisonment had lost its desired result."

The *Anderson* and *Lawrence* cases emphasize that legitimate Asset Protection Planning utilizing Off Shore Trusts is not for perpetuators of fraud or individuals who are obviously already insolvent (because they are judgment debtors or have substantial legitimate claims ready to be or already asserted against them). The other factor, however, highlighted by the *Lawrence* and *Anderson* cases, is that the establishment of Offshore Trusts needs to be carefully monitored and implemented under legitimate conditions by a competent, trustworthy, and knowledgeable attorney.

Offshore Modular Planning

The modular planning discussed in association with the DAPT (and shown in Figure 10.1) is equally applicable to Offshore Planning. The difference is, of course, that the FAPT is a foreign-based Trust, and often the LLCs are Offshore LLCs. For example, let's assume that Steve Mason is a successful real estate developer. Over the years, he has accumulated a great deal of liquidity as a result of arranging some very successful real estate projects. Because he deals with investors, and because he is concerned about potential liability with respect to his real estate projects, he decides to establish a Cook Islands Asset Protection Trust for the benefit of himself, his wife, and his children. He selects a Cook Islands Trust company to be the Trustee of the Trust, and an offshore company to act as the Protector of the Trust.

In planning his offshore structure with his knowledgeable attorney, Steve elects to set up a Nevis LLC and an Anguilla LLC—which will be owned 90% each by *his* Cook Islands Trust and 10% each by a Cook Islands Trust set up exclusively for his children. His Nevis LLC opens a bank account offshore, and Steve funds the account with a substantial monetary deposit.

Steve utilizes his other offshore LLC to be the parent of a Costa Rican LLC which owns a beach-front condo that Steve rents out and also uses for family vacations. Steve also elects to set up a Nevada DAPT which is the owner of several LLCs that hold the title to many of Steve's real estate projects.

By utilizing this modular planning, Steve has substantially protected most of his assets and erected a strong fortress to withstand the onslaught of potential creditor attacks.

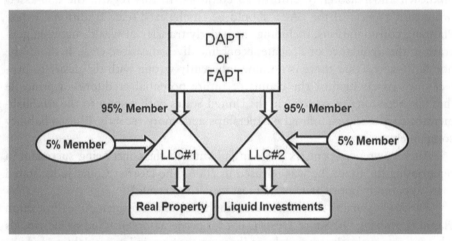

Figure 10.1. The Modular Structuring Diagram (See also p. 52, Chapter 9)

CHAPTER

11

Advanced Estate Planning Techniques

Once the fundamental Estate Planning structure has been put in place, and Business and Asset Protection Levels (previously discussed) have been analyzed, structured, and established to implement the recommended plan of action, business owners and professionals should then focus on some Advanced Estate Planning Techniques that will help meet their estate, income tax, and legacy placing.

The Irrevocable Life Insurance Trust

Irrevocable Life Insurance Trusts (ILITs) have been utilized by estate planners for several decades. An ILIT is a Trust that is set up and established for purposes of owning a life insurance policy on the life of the Trustor or Settlor of the Trust. The Trust pays the premiums to keep the insurance in force, collects the death benefits upon the insured's death and distributes the money according to the terms of the Trust. Because the insured does not own the insurance (the Trust does), the life insurance proceeds are not included in the insured's estate for purposes of estate taxes. The insured determines the Trust terms when it is set up, but since the Trust is irrevocable, it cannot be amended. The ILIT is an excellent way to provide for heirs, and to avoid estate taxes.

Each year, the Trustor or maker of the Trust can make a gift to the Trust in the amount of the annual exclusion ($14,000) per beneficiary, without having to pay gift taxes or use any of the gift tax credit. This gifted amount can be utilized to make the premium payments on the insurance policies. Each year, the Trustee will be notified that the premium is due and the Trustee then needs to coordinate with the

ILITs are very popular vehicles to provide beneficiaries with liquidity upon the death of the Trustor and help pay estate taxes.

Settlor with respect to his or her deposit into the Trust bank account of the annual premium amount. Concurrently therewith, the Trustee needs to send out notices to the beneficiaries ("the Crummy Letter") advising them that they have the right to take their proportionate share of the premium out of the account if they desire. The reason they have to have this right and that the letter has to be sent is because in order to take advantage of the annual per donee exclusion, the donee has to have a present interest in the gift proceeds.

Many estate planners utilize the ILIT for purposes of providing liquidity upon the death of the Trustor in order to pay estate taxes or to provide liquid funds to the beneficiaries. However, an additional benefit of the ILIT is the Asset Protection feature. As long as the set-up of the Trust and the transfer of the premium funds are not considered to be a fraudulent conveyance, creditors of the Trustor cannot get to the proceeds of the insurance. This then, is an excellent technique for a parent to utilize in order to protect the inheritance of his or her children, or other beneficiaries.

Family Limited Partnerships and LLCs

A Family Limited Partnership (FLP) or Limited Liability Company (LLC) is typically utilized in an Estate Plan as a vehicle for making "leveraged" or "discounted" gifts to children or other family members and loved ones. The FLP or Family Limited Liability Company (FLLC) is, simply stated, a partnership arrangement between family members, wherein the senior family members (1) maintain full control over the management and investment decisions relating to all of the underlying partnership property and (2) make gifts to the junior family members of the limited partner or LLC interest on a discounted basis.

The limited partners or non-senior LLC members do not have any voice in the management of the entity. Most FLPs and FLLCs are also structured to provide that the limited partners or members will not be allowed to transfer their partnership or member interest during their lifetime without the consent of the other partners/members. This restriction on the transfer of the limited partner/member interest, along with other factors, provides for the discount of the value of the gifted partnership interest for gift tax purposes by reducing its marketability (Marketability Discount). Because the limited partners/members do not have any voice in the management of the partnership, the value of the gifted limited partner interest will be discounted to reflect the lack of control (Control Discount). Combining these two discounts is sometimes referred to jointly as a Minority Discount and typically reduces the value of the transfer gift for gift tax purposes by 20–50%.

The senior family members can take control of the partnership property for as long as they desire. The Minority Discount of the value of the limited partnership/LLC member interest allows the transfer to effectively make large annual gifts without utilizing as much of the gift tax credit as would otherwise be mandated. For example, with a real estate FLP or FLLC, the discount can be as much as 30–50%.

The benefit with respect to utilizing FLPs or FLLCs from an Asset Protection standpoint is the Charging Order protection that a creditor of the limited partner/LLC member is limited to, as explained in Chapter 5.

Charitable Remainder Trusts and Charitable Lead Trusts

Charitable Trusts may be set up either during a donor's life or as part of the Trust or Will after death. Charitable Remainder Trusts (CRTs) are Irrevocable Trusts established by a Trustor/Donor to provide an income to the income beneficiary while the charity or private foundation receives the remainder value of the Trust principal when the Trust terminates, normally upon the Trustor's death. The Donor/Trustor may claim a charitable income tax deduction upon funding the Trust and can also avoid paying a capital gain tax when highly appreciated assets such as stock or real estate are transferred to the Trust. Therefore, the set-up of the CRT can result in a reduction of income tax now and estate taxes upon death, and there is no capital gain tax when the asset is sold. In addition, of course, it is one way to benefit a preferred charity.

TIP

A Charitable Remainder Trust provides income to a beneficiary while the Donor/Trustor is still alive; a donation of the principal to the selected charity upon the death of the Donor/Trustor; a charitable income tax deduction when funding the Trust; and avoidance of capital gains tax when appreciated assets are transferred to the Trust.

The other benefit of the CRT is in the form of Asset Protection. The transfer to the Trust preserves the Trust asset from creditor attack. Often, the establishment of the CRT is combined with an ILIT for maximum Estate Planning benefits. The income tax savings and part of the income received from the CRT can be utilized to pay the insurance premiums for the ILIT. The Trustee of the ILIT can then purchase enough life insurance to replace the full value of the asset for the benefit of the Trustor's children or other beneficiaries.

A Charitable Lead Trust (CLT) differs from the CRT in that the present income of the CLT is distributed to charities. After a specified period of time, the remainder is passed to the noncharitable beneficiaries of the CLT. The main idea of the CLT is to provide tax savings while still allowing for an ultimate distribution to heirs.

Grantor Retained Annuity Trust

A Grantor Retained Annuity Trust or "GRAT" is a Trust arrangement utilized by more wealthy individuals to engender estate tax savings. The Trustor/Donor sets up the GRAT and then makes a donation to it. In return, the GRAT pays the

Trustor an annual annuity payment for a fixed period of time. At the end of the term, any remaining assets in the GRAT are passed on to the beneficiary of the Trust as a gift. To experience the tax benefit, the sum of the scheduled annuity payment of the GRAT equals a part of the principal plus interest. The strategy is that the principal will increase in value and that the minimum interest paid to the donor will be less than the appreciation, and any interest earned by the Trust. The remaining values are passed on to the beneficiary without incurring any gift tax. Once again, the assets inside the GRAT are protected from creditors.

Qualified Personal Residence Trust

A Qualified Personal Residence Trust or "QPRT" can be a technique to not only save estate taxes, but also asset protect a principal residence. A QPRT is an irrevocable split-interest Trust. The split-interest character of the Trust is based on the right of the grantor's to live in the residence for a number of years rent free; then, the beneficiaries of the Trust become the owners of the residence. Because the donor retains an interest, the value of the transfer or gift to the Trust has to be reduced to take into account the life interest retained by the grantor. Again, the QPRT can be an effective tool for Asset Protection Planning because the transfer of the residence to the Trust is complete and should be protected from creditors absent a finding of fraudulent conveyance.

The Intentionally Defective Irrevocable Trust

Many people can enhance the benefits of a traditional Revocable Trust plan by adding an Irrevocable Trust. Whereas the Revocable Trust can avoid Probate costs and reduce some estate taxes, the Irrevocable Trust can allow for the long-term growth of all assets without estate or gift taxes. Properly designed Irrevocable Trusts can even help grandchildren and other future beneficiaries receive assets without generation-skipping taxes. For these reasons, Irrevocable Trusts are often called Dynasty Trusts. Probably the most powerful and popular Irrevocable Trust used in advanced tax planning is the Intentionally Defective Irrevocable Trust (IDIT). Zero-tax plans frequently include IDITs because they can provide the most efficient use of a client's gift and estate tax exemption. For example, if the exemption is $5 million, a client can gift the $5 million tax free from the taxable estate to the IDIT. This gift gives the IDIT economic substance. The IDIT Trust can then buy real estate, securities, or even businesses from the taxable estate in exchange for a note. If a growth asset is put into an LLC or similar entity before the sale, the entity may be discounted so that the value is "squeezed." Once the taxable estate sells the asset for a note, it is possible to freeze the value of the note or even design the note to have no value at a future point. Such a "squeeze-freeze" technique helps stabilize or decrease the value of the taxable estate while accumulating substantial value in a Trust that is free from estate taxes. IDITs can achieve many nontax goals as well. For example, clients like to tell potential creditors or divorcing spouses that they do not own any assets. This can be true if assets are held in an Irrevocable Trust. Moreover, experienced attorneys can design IDITs to transfer ownership, management, and control to heirs in the right way at the right time in a way that honors the values of the family establishing the IDIT. The IDIT rewards the pursuit of nontax goals with four significant tax benefits. First, the IDIT helps a client avoid estate taxes by moving assets out of an estate to a Trust where assets can appreciate without any estate tax on the growth. Second, IDITs avoid gift taxes because the proper sale of an asset to a Defective Trust is not a gift. Third, IDITs avoid capital gains taxes because the IRS disregards sales to Defective Trusts when calculating income taxes. Fourth, when the sale is completed, the client will usually take back an interest-bearing note to provide lifetime income. Given the defective nature of the IDIT Trust, the note "interest" need not be subject to the ordinary income taxes normally assessed on interest. Payments on IDIT notes may be paid as capital gains income or even tax-free distributions, depending on the type of income produced by assets in the IDIT Trust.

New estate, gift and generation skipping transfer exemptions and rates were introduced under the American Taxpayer Relief Act of 2012 ("ATRA"). Now the top rate for the estate, gift, and GST tax is 40%. The estate, gift, and GST credit equivalent or tax exemption has been raised to $5 million and indexed for inflation using a 2011 base line which means that the exemption for 2015 is $5,430,000. A married couple can then pass $10,860,000 without incurring any federal estate tax liability. However, a few states still have an estate or inheritance tax, and so individual taxpayers have to take that into consideration in their Estate Planning.

Now, at the federal level, a 20% rate is applied for long-term capital gains and qualified dividends for taxpayers in the top tax bracket. The 3.8% net investment income (Obamacare Tax) and any state income tax will be extra. Accordingly, the effective capital gains tax rate for high income individuals can be well in excess of 30%. What this means is that deciding whether to make lifetime gifts by creating irrevocable Trusts involves more careful weighing of the loss of the step-up in basis, shifting of income, and other factors. Income tax planning is back in the limelight and it is important for persons of affluence to have an integrated approach to their estate, income tax, and Asset Protection Planning.

Just What the Doctor Ordered

Some Special Issues and Strategies for Physicians and Dentists

Over the years, I have had the privilege of working with and representing several physicians with respect to their business, tax, estate, and Asset Protection Planning needs and objectives. Contrary to the experience of some of my colleagues, for the most part, I have found the doctor–lawyer relationship to be a very enjoyable and satisfying one.

Obviously, as a general rule, doctors don't like lawyers. There are a few manifest reasons for this. First of all, a malpractice lawsuit brought by a lawyer is the physician's worst nightmare. Secondly, most lawyers don't make an effort to appreciate and understand their physician client's practice and the time and pressure constraints it engenders. Physicians are, obviously, bright and have put significant time and effort into the medical education process; yet, many lawyers don't give full faith and credit to the physician's background and operating practice.

Actually, I think an attorney's approach to the way he or she represents clients should be similar to a physician's treatment of a patient. For instance: A client comes to me with a legal, tax, or business problem. I try to gather the necessary information so I can understand the client (patient) and his or her concerns. I probe to identify the specific areas of need (identify the symptoms). Once I have done that, I can make a diagnosis and follow that up with a designed strategy (remedy/plan of care). I then perform the services and implement the strategies just as the physician would in addressing the health condition of the patient. Finally, I follow up and make sure that the client's plan is properly maintained, and I recommend and schedule regular meetings with the client (checkups). I also prescribe various steps (medications) that can be taken to keep the client's legal and business health in good shape.

Don't get me wrong—a physician's practice often deals with life-and-death situations and has much more acute personal consequences than my legal services. I recognize that and have only the highest regard and respect for the physicians' skill and health-saving and -promoting service. At the same time, however, what I do has a dramatic impact on my client's financial well-being and even their ability to relax and sleep better at night.

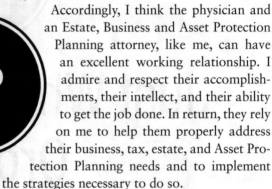

Physicians are advised to practice as an independent contractor and form a Professional Medical Corp. The medical equipment should be held in an LLC and the LLC can lease the equipment back to the medical practice.

Accordingly, I think the physician and an Estate, Business and Asset Protection Planning attorney, like me, can have an excellent working relationship. I admire and respect their accomplishments, their intellect, and their ability to get the job done. In return, they rely on me to help them properly address their business, tax, estate, and Asset Protection Planning needs and to implement the strategies necessary to do so.

I have chosen to include this special chapter to highlight the unique challenges physicians/dentists face. At the same time, however, all of the other chapters in this book relate to them as well, as evidenced by the included fact situations involving healthcare providers. (In my experience, a majority of books by Estate and Asset Protection Planning lawyers, written exclusively for physicians and dentists, tend to be either overly simplistic, or somewhat patronizing and condescending. In some cases, they are much too general, and in other cases, they are designed to sell a product, not a service. This book is neither. It is designed to help professionals understand Asset Protection Planning and nothing more. Even after reading this book, the physician/dentist would still need to have his or her practice and personal financial situations personally reviewed and strategized by a competent Estate and Asset Protection attorney.)

Each of the elements of a physicians' practice below can be extended for Dentists and other oral healthcare professionals. For the sake of brevity, I refer to just a few types of situations that parallel multiple circumstances.

The Medical Practice

There are myriad ways in which physicians practice medicine. Some are employed exclusively by hospitals and/or Surgical Centers, either as employees or independent contractors. Some own and operate their own medical practice, either as sole practitioners or as part of a medical group or clinic. Each different practice situation is unique, and it cannot be pigeonholed into a cookie-cutter-type structure. That being said, there are some specific guidelines and salient points that can be relevant to every practice structure.

1. Independent Contractor

It is normally advantageous for a physician to practice as an independent contractor rather than as an employee. As an independent contractor, the physician can incorporate as a Professional Medical Corporation and may be better able to structure his or her income for income tax savings and other related business benefits. In this regard, the establishment of the physician's own medical corporation may help to limit his or her malpractice exposure from other physicians, medical personnel, and service providers with whom the physician works. This arrangement can also provide some flexibility and financial planning opportunities that would otherwise not be available as an employee or as a partner.

2. Equipment

If the physician has his or her own practice or is in a practice with other physicians, the medical equipment of the practice should be held in a separate LLC. The LLC can then lease the equipment to the practice—whether it be the medical corporation of the sole practitioner, or the group clinic, or Surgical Center.

3. Professional Relationship Agreements

Many younger physicians find themselves buying into a practice, while more senior physicians are involved in selling an interest or all of their practice to the more junior physician. Some physicians work together either as a medical group or clinic; a few more entrepreneurial physicians are involved in setting up and operating Surgical Centers. All of these situations require carefully drafted and well-thought-out agreements and contracts carefully delineating the rights and duties of the parties.

Recently, I had the opportunity of representing a more junior doctor buying into a very well-established practice. There were several very critical issues that had to be addressed from the standpoint of my client and the physician with the existing practice. There were four different agreements involved—including an employment agreement for each of the doctors, a shareholder agreement, and the buy-in agreement. This was not an exercise for the inexperienced; both I and my counter-part had an extensive background in these types of agreements and relationships. The result, after many negotiations and give-and-take, was a structure that has proven to be mutually beneficial for both physicians.

4. Surgical Center

The Surgical Center is a stand-alone medical facility that provides physicians with the necessary equipment and medical environment to perform a variety of less-acute medical procedures and operations. Normally, the Surgical Center is run and operated by a Professional Medical Corporation with a chief operating physician at its head. The Surgical Center facility is either owned or leased by an LLC. Usually, the LLC is a turnkey operation that owns all of the equipment and fixtures, and leases the building and equipment to the medical operating corporation. If the Surgical Center LLC does not own the building for the facility, it leases it, and then stocks it with the equipment and fixtures. It then subleases the resultant product to the operating entity. Nonphysician investors can be members of the LLC in this arrangement. This is a very technical area and needs very exacting legal guidance with respect to the setup and structure of the Surgical Center.

Malpractice

Why Should Doctors Worry?

Even though physicians/dentists face uncertain times with respect to revenue production, the generation and earnings of physicians and dentists are among the highest of any occupation.

The public's perception of them is that they are affluent and have readily accessible "deep pockets." Accordingly, their planning needs exceed traditional solutions.

Because physicians/dentists have significant income from their practices, they often leverage their income by purchasing real estate investment properties and setting up securities accounts for more liquid investments such as stocks, bonds, and mutual funds. They also participate in an equity basis in related product services and other businesses. Accordingly, they need the protection discussed in Chapter 8 with respect to reliability-protected entities. Each of their real estate investments and their stock/investment accounts should be placed into separate or joint LLCs. The LLC member interests, in turn, can be owned by a Domestic or Foreign Asset Protection Trust.

Doctors and Dentists are at high risk for malpractice claims. Over the last several decades, expanding theories of liability and aggressive plaintiff lawyers have markedly increased the chances of adverse medical malpractice judgments. The victim-oriented society we live in, with the perverse nature of the deep-pocket theory, enables plaintiffs to loom as menacing predators against the physician/dentist. Moreover, because of the increased media and social awareness—and the high notoriety created for malpractice and other errors-and-omissions types of action—physicians/dentists are likely targets for losses, whether or not these claims have strong merit.

Non-Practice Assets and Investments

Many physicians have been able to acquire personal assets and investments such as rental real estate, brokerage accounts, and various other financial interests. Moreover, most physicians have personal residences of substantial value. All of these assets need to be protected to the greatest extent possible and also need to be part of a well-thought-out and implemented Estate Plan.

At this point, certain case studies and hypothetical situations that have been set forth in other chapters of this book may be consulted. For example, see Hypothetical Case Study No. 3 on page 54, the John White Case Study on page 14, and the Step One example on page 23.

As has been pointed out in Chapter 8, all rental and commercial reality should be held in separate LLCs. The LLC gives protection to the physician owner from claims against the property itself. These claims are restricted to the property within the LLC and cannot be asserted against other assets of the owner. Moreover, in the event of a malpractice suit or personal claims against the physician, the LLC provides the additional benefit of the Charging Order protection. However, setting up an LLC for an investment or real estate asset is not enough. It is strongly recommended that the physician utilize either a DAPT or a FAPT to own the member interest of the LLC. For physicians in California, a Private Retirement Plan may also be an extremely viable Asset Protection alternative, as the assets within the Plan are exempt from creditors.

The physician's personal residence cannot be placed inside an LLC, as has been explained previously, because there is no business purpose behind such transfer. The physician should equity strip the personal residence to the extent possible (keeping in mind the practicality of serving the debt). Most physicians are in a position where they can take out a substantial home equity line of credit. This is an essential part of a strong Asset Protection Plan. The line of credit does not have to be drawn upon unless the situation warrants it. In the meantime, it acts as a deterrent by reducing, on paper at least, the equity in the residence, and it can provide much-needed funds in the event of a lawsuit attack against the physician.

Conclusion

Physicians and dentists are at great risk because they are an attractive target. A disappointed or disgruntled patient can always second-guess the decisions of the healthcare provider. The deep-pocket theory is readily applicable to these professionals because the general public thinks of them as somewhat elitist and well off. Doctors and dentists have worked hard to achieve their professional standing and put in long and stressful hours with respect to their practice. They deserve the same high quality of legal and business care that they give as healthcare providers. I like the analogy one surgeon gave me in talking about how he selected an Estate and Asset Protection Planning attorney. He said, "Just as you would want the most capable and experienced surgeon available for your operation, I want the best and most experienced attorney to implement my Estate and Asset Protection Plan." Experience, skill, and track record is: "Just What the Doctor Ordered."

CHAPTER

13

Climbing the Ladder and Putting It All Together

In the previous chapters of this book, we have discussed the various steps on the Ladder of Success with respect to the design, implementation, and maintenance of a successful Estate and Asset Protection Plan. Now that the reader has a basic understanding of what is involved in putting together a program that protects and preserves assets, we must examine how one goes about initiating and implementing the process.

Action 1

The first and most crucial step is to find the right attorney and advisor who can help design and implement the plan. The attorney should be very knowledgeable in both Estate and Asset Protection Planning, in addition to having a good background in business and tax planning. Personal references should be sought out from other advisors, such as CPAs and financial planners, and the internet can be partially utilized to find and verify the expertise of the attorney with whom you choose to work. Here are some helpful hints with respect to selecting the proper attorney:

- The attorney should have substantial experience in the Estate, Asset Protection, and Business Planning areas. This degree of expertise should be reflected by the years he or she has practiced, the attorney's background and training, and the attorney's reputation for competency and ethics.
- The attorney should have the proper network and contacts with Trust companies, corporate and LLC agents, bank officers, and other contacts relative to the design and structure of the plan.

- The attorney should be an acknowledged leader in his or her field—as indicated by his or her background and training, experience, and authorship of relevant legal Articles and publications. It is a major plus if the attorney has experience in teaching and making presentations to law students, financial advisors and CPAs, and even more importantly, to other attorneys, as that ensures he or she is adept at communication. Attorneys need to take Continuing Education courses to keep their licenses current, and the State Bar Association and other continuing legal education providers select top-notch attorneys to give continuing legal education presentations during courses. It is advisable to find one good enough to have been asked.
- There are two major attorney-rating services. Martindale Hubble is the oldest and most prestigious rating service. It rates lawyers nationally and internationally and sponsors the Websites Lawyers.com and Attorneys.com. The highest rating Martindale Hubble gives is "A" for competency and "V" for ethics. Therefore, Martindale Hubble's rating of "AV" is its most excellent rating. The other attorney rating service (AVVO) is relatively new, but has climbed to the top, where it is now the equal of Martindale Hubble. The AVVO rating is numerical, and a 10/10 rating of "Superb" is its highest rating. Both Martindale Hubble and AVVO have strict due-diligence and procedural guidelines for assessing lawyers, and deriving a rating for them.
- There are other factors that should be examined when choosing an attorney, which include client testimonials, other attorney endorsements, and achievement awards—both in the legal profession and otherwise.
- Finally, and, perhaps most importantly, clients should have a complete feeling of trust and goodwill toward the attorney they select. They need to feel confident about the attorney's ability to tailor the plan to their particular needs and to watch their backside. The attorney needs to work well with their other professional advisors and demonstrate a caring concern for the clients and their families. The attorney's staff should reflect this caring attitude and make a genuine impression on the client that they, their plan, and its structure are very, very important, and deserve the utmost professionalism, responsiveness, and hands-on attentiveness.

CAUTION

Don't select an attorney out of the Yellow Pages. Put time and effort into the selection process. Pay particular attention to whether your prospective attorney teaches, or has published Articles on the subject matter.

Action 2

Once a client has selected the attorney with whom he or she is pleased to work, the next step is to work with the attorney and the client's other professional advisors in designing and establishing the plan. All of the various steps on the ladder need to be addressed. As we have already discussed, some of the levels are more important and relevant for some individuals than for others. Each of the levels, however, should be examined and analyzed for pertinence.

It is important in arriving at the proper plan and design that the attorney and other professional advisors have complete access to all of a client's financial and personal information. The attorney must know and understand what the client's business interests are, how he or she holds title to those assets and what the client's personal situation is with respect to health, marriage, family and other important interests and concerns.

Action 3

Once a client has provided all the information, and his or her attorney and/or advisors have devised the plan, the next step is, of course, to implement the plan. The implementation is mainly the attorney's job: rafting the Trust, setting up, and drafting the legal entities and other legal documents that are part of that individual's particular plan. A client's involvement, however, remains critical because he or she needs to be available and provide the necessary information to the attorney regarding the establishment of the plan. The attorney will generally do most of the work, but the client is still involved in making decisions, executing documents and funding the entities and Trust involved. Often, the funding aspects of the plan are neglected. As mentioned earlier, the plan is really not efficacious unless the proper funding occurs with respect to depositing the relevant assets into the appropriate entities and Trust.

Action 4

Once the plan is instituted and properly set up and organized, it must be properly maintained. Often, it is a good idea to enter into a maintenance agreement with the attorney, whereby the attorney can provide ongoing maintenance services to make sure the plan stays properly compliant and legally intact. The maintenance program will often require that the attorney interact with the client's CPA and/or other professional advisors about tax reporting and funding.

Hypothetical Case Studies

To conclude our discussion, we will examine two different case studies to help bring the principles that have been discussed throughout the book together in an applicable and relevant circumstance. These case studies are not intended to be exhaustive and all-encompassing. No one should apply any of the recommendations made in this book without consulting a competent attorney. Readers need specific legal advice in order to properly structure and tailor a plan that meets their unique needs and objectives.

Case Study A

Dr. Harry Hands is a licensed physician who has specialized in cosmetic surgery. He was recently affiliated with a medical group but has since ventured out on his own. He has not incorporated but has a working relationship with a Surgical Center operated by a group of other plastic surgeons and anesthesiologists.

Dr. Hands is 42 years old and his wife, Priscilla Prudent, is 40. The couple have two minor children, ages 13 and 10. Their personal financial statement reads as follows:

Assets

Residence:	Fair market value of $2,000,000 less $500,000 mortgage
Vacation Home:	$1,500,000 fair market value
Residential Rental Property:	$1,000,000 less $400,000 mortgage
Pension Plan:	Harry: $350,000
IRA:	Priscilla: $50,000

Securities at Morgan Stanley

Smith Barney:	$500,000
Harry's Professional Practice:	$500,000 ($150,000 of which is equipment)
Liabilities:	Business Line of Credit: $150,000
	Credit Card Debt: $175,000

Dr. Hands and Pricilla are interested in Asset Protection Planning. Dr. Hands has recently had difficulty obtaining malpractice insurance because of previous litigation that has now been settled.

Possible Recommendations

- Dr. Hands needs to address the structure of his professional practice and should probably set up a Professional Medical Corporation in which to conduct his medical practice. It is vitally important that he incorporates in order to protect himself from liability relative to both—the other plastic surgeons and anesthesiologists with whom he works, as well as to the Surgical Center. There may also be some residual tax benefits on account of setting up the Professional Corporation.
- Obviously, Dr. Hands and his wife, Pricilla, need to be concerned about some basic Estate Planning. They have minor children, and it is critically important that they address the issues set forth in Chapter 6, such as a Revocable Living Trust, Pour-Over Wills, Durable Powers of Attorney, Healthcare Directives, and other legal documents.
- At the very least, Dr. Hands' equipment should be placed in a separate LLC, independent from his Professional Corporation.
- Dr. Hands' vacation home and residential rental property should probably be placed in separate LLCs.
- Dr. Hands' pension plan is exempt from creditors as long as he is not the sole beneficiary of the plan. Pricilla's IRA is probably protected both under bankruptcy law and most state laws.
- Dr. Hands should consider placing his securities at Morgan Stanley in an LLC.

- Dr. Hands and Pricilla should consider setting up a DAPT to hold title to the member interests of their LLCs and also to their residence.
- Dr. Hands and Pricilla should consider entering into a maintenance agreement with their attorney to assist them in complying with proper state requirements, coordinating matters with their CPA and professional advisors, and keeping their plan up-to-date.

Case Study B

Jose and Claudia Santos are in their late sixties. They are native Filipino, but are now naturalized US Citizens. They have been very successful in purchasing various real estate parcels in the Southern California area, upon two of which they have constructed and now operate successful convalescent hospital (CH) operations. They have two adult children, a daughter and one son. The daughter and her husband are both involved in the convalescent hospital businesses. The son is a successful business litigation attorney. Jose and Claudia's personal financial statement shows the following:

Assets

Residence:	Fair market value $1,500,000, no mortgage
Vacation Condo in Palm Desert:	Fair market value $800,000, no mortgage
Commercial Rental Property (Independent of convalescent hospital):	Fair market value $3,000,000, Mortgage: $1,000,000
Property in Philippines:	Value $250,000
Liquid funds at HSBC:	$5,000,000
Securities at Merrill Lynch	$2,000,000

Convalescent Hospital (CH)

CH #1, Corporation:	Value unknown
CH #2, Corporation:	Value unknown
CH #3, Corporation:	Value unknown
CH real estate #1:	Value $3,500,000, mortgage $1,500,000
CH real estate #2:	Value $4,750,000, mortgage $3,000,000
CH real estate #3:	leased from 3rd party

Jose and Claudia are interested in selling at least one and maybe two of the CHs within the next several months. Their daughter and son-in-law want to keep the third CH and eventually own and operate it.

Preliminary Comments

Jose and Claudia may be candidates for an offshore structure, as they have property in the Philippines and probably have other family members there.

Moreover and most importantly, they have substantial liquid funds that can be placed offshore.

Recommendations

- The first step is to review and analyze the corporations that operate the convalescent hospitals. The corporations should be examined for compliance: that Minutes and Resolutions are being kept up and that shareholder loans have been properly documented.
- Jose and Claudia need to ensure that their fundamental Estate Planning is in order. For a review of this, see Chapter 6.
- If CH Corporations Nos. 1, 2, and 3 are S Corporations, it may be advisable to spin off the property and equipment of the hospitals and place them in separate LLCs, which, in turn, can then rent the equipment back to the corporations.
- The vacation condo, the commercial rental property, and CH real estate Nos. 1 and 2 should all be placed in separate LLCs, if this has not already been done.
- Jose and Claudia should consider setting up a Cook Islands Asset Protection Trust and at least two or three offshore LLCs to be owned by the Trust. Some of their liquid funds and securities can be placed in the offshore LLCs, and one of the offshore LLCs can own the entity that owns the property in the Philippines.
- Jose and Claudia should probably also set up a DAPT to hold the title to their residence and the LLCs that own their domestic real estate.
- Since they want to pass CH Corporation No. 2 to their daughter and son-in-law, it may be appropriate to enter into a gift-making program now for gifting the stock of the corporation and, perhaps, the member interest of the LLC that owns the convalescent property for which the corporation is doing business.
- Jose and Claudia should enter into a maintenance agreement with their attorney in order to make sure (1) that all of their entities stay legally compliant and (2) that there is coordination between them, their CPA, and their attorney.

Conclusion

The purpose of this book is not to give readers a self-help guide to preserving and protecting assets. Instead, what I have tried to do is to provide a fundamental description of the various issues of Asset Protection so that readers can then have a better understanding of the strategies and techniques involved in Asset Protection Planning. This will assist them in searching for their optimal solution. These strategies and techniques must be designed and implemented by a knowledgeable attorney with assistance from experienced and well-regarded financial advisors and CPAs. Hopefully, you as readers will now have more incentive and desire to put your own Estate and Asset Protection Plan into action—the earlier, the better.

Remember...

One of the important factors that should stand out to you after reading this book is that everyone is different and needs his or her own individualized plan. Here are some of the main differences that should be properly noted:

- What are the risks? Obviously, professional service providers such as physicians, dentists, attorneys, CPAs, and other professionals who are subject to claims of malpractice are greatly at risk; so are sellers of businesses, anyone who solicits money from investors, business and real estate owners, and individuals who have to sign personal guarantees and lending documents. A more complete list of those at risk is found in Chapter 2. The more risk you face, the more you need to properly prepare and set up a well-structured Asset Protection Plan.

- What is your lifestyle and culture? Are you married or single? Do you have children? If so, are they minors or adults? Is your marriage stable, and are you and your spouse fully invested in it?

- What is your net worth, and what are your assets? This is a question I always ask our clients: What assets do you have that you wish to protect? Many people have assets tied up in their business. Others have substantial investment assets. Many people have large real estate holdings but little liquidity. All of these issues have to be examined in order to properly design and tailor the best Estate and Asset Protection Plan.

- In what state do you reside? This is important because state law defines property rights and exemptions. Are you in a community property state or a separate property state? Do you have tenancy by the entirety? What are the assets exempted from creditor attack in your estate? What are the homestead exemption laws?

- Who are your heirs, and do you have charitable desires? Are you interested in passing your assets on to your children? Are you concerned about children-in-laws and potential creditors of your children? Do you have elderly parents for whom you are concerned? Do any of your loved ones have special needs?

- Are you in a position to make offshore planning a viable alternative? Do you have substantial liquid assets that can be moved offshore? Do you have relatives or friends offshore? Do you have offshore business interests or investments? How great are the risks you face?

Obviously, there are myriad other individual characteristics that need to be taken into account in designing and setting up a strategy and Asset Protection Plan. Also note that your Asset Protection Plan should always be part of your overall Estate Plan. The strategies you adopt should tie into and be part of the plan you have for transferring your legacy to the next generation.

Finally, in closing, I want to again express my profound admiration and respect for those of you readers who have been out on the frontlines of your business and profession. Thank you for your contributions, your sacrifices, and your dedication. I know what it took for you to accomplish what you have, and I hope that you will be able to preserve and protect what you have worked so hard to build.

Business Entity Checklist

1. Identify each of the principals. For *each*, gather the following information:
   - Name
   - Address
   - Telephone number
   - Social Security Number
   - Relationship to other principals, if any
2. For *each* principal, obtain the following data:
   - Name
   - Net worth
   - Income from sources outside the venture in question
   - Anticipated salary or other compensation to be paid from business
   - Anticipated fringe benefits from business
3. Obtain the following data with respect to the business itself:
   - Description of business
   - Management of business
   - Significant risk of operation of business
   - Any particular licensing requirements
   - Location

- Necessity for protection of intellectual property, i.e., patents, copyrights, trademarks, etc.
- Any types of contract that corporation will initially have to enter into, i.e., franchise, distributorship, employment contracts

4. Determine the relationship of the business to any other business entity, if any. Specifically, determine:
   - Is the business related to any other business entity? How?
   - Is it a successor or affiliate of any business entity?
5. Determine the likelihood of potential sale of business in the future.
6. Evaluate if the business will likely be a candidate for public offering.
7. Evaluate capital needs:
   - Initial capital requirements
   - Long-term capital requirements
   - Alternative means of raising capital
   - Allocation of ownership interest
   - Allocation of cash flow
   - Loans and other third-party investments
   - Transfer of assets
   - Necessity of personal guarantees

APPENDIX

B

LLC Explanation

1. What is a Limited Liability Company?

A limited liability company or "LLC" is a business entity that is authorized by specific legislation in most states of the United States and in many foreign countries. In almost every instance, the state or country in question issues a charter to the LLC upon its formation. The most significant characteristic possessed by LLCs is, as the name suggests, that it provides limited liability. In this regard, it is very similar to a corporation.

2. How Do You Form an LLC?

An LLC is formed by filing the Articles of Organization with the relevant Secretary of State in the US or other licensing agency in a foreign country. The Articles of Organization are normally very brief and simple and provide only basic information with respect to the name of the company, the agent for service of process, the company's address and its manager or members.

3. How Is an LLC Structured?

An LLC is structured much like a partnership except that it has members instead of partners. The LLC can be member-managed in a manner similar to a General Partnership, or it can be Manager-managed just as a General Partner manages a limited partnership. If the LLC is Member-managed, normally, all of the members have an equal vote and decide between themselves on not only the major business and financial policies, but also the everyday operations. If the LLC is Manager-managed, the members only decide on major financial and business decisions, and the Manager handles all of the day-to-day business operations.

4. How Is the Structure of the LLC Determined?

The founding members or promoters of the LLC determine the structure of the LLC by means of an Operating Agreement, which is similar to a Partnership Agreement. Normally, when the Articles of Organization are filed, the state requires that the organizers determine in the Articles whether or not the LLC is Member-managed or Manager-managed. The members have an experienced attorney draft the Operating Agreement that sets forth the different rights and responsibilities of the members and covers matters such as capital contributions, division of profits, management, member meetings, transfers of member interests, dissolution and indemnification.

5. What Are the On-Going State Fees for an LLC?

California imposes an $800 Annual Franchise Tax on LLCs. This amount is due on the 15th day of the fourth month after the beginning of the fiscal year. For the first year, the due date is the 15th day of the fourth month from the date the LLC was organized. In addition, California, in its arrogance, also imposes a gross receipts tax on LLCs. For LLCs whose annual revenue is between $250,000 and $499,999, the additional fee is $900. The fee increases to $2,500 for annual revenues between $500,000 and $999,999, $6,000 for annual revenues between $1 million and $499,999, and $11,790 for annual revenues of $5 million or more.

6. What Are the Tax and Accounting Procedures?

A multi-member LLC can elect to be taxed as either a partnership or a corporation. Almost always it is better to be taxed as a partnership. What this means is that the LLC files an Information Return and issues K-1 forms to its members showing the member's share of the income or loss that the LLC incurs. The members then report this amount on their own individual Returns. The LLC, if it is taxed like a partnership, does not pay any income tax. If the LLC is a single-member LLC, the owner may treat it as a disregarded entity for tax purposes and report the tax and related accounting on the individual tax return of the member. This eliminates the necessity of a tax return for the LLC.

7. What is the Charging Order?

A Charging Order is a court order available to a judgment creditor directed to an LLC or limited partnership of which the judgment debtor is a member or partner.

This grants the judgment creditor the right to whatever distributions would otherwise be due to the debtor member/partner whose interest is being charged. The purpose of the Charging Order is to prevent the judgment creditor of an individual partner/member from access to the partnership/LLC assets, while at the same time giving the creditor some relief relative to distributions from the entity to the partner/member. The Charging Order denies the creditor direct access to the LLC assets; it limits the creditor exclusively to collection of the income or distributions that the LLC assets might engender, but which can be withheld from distribution at the discretion of the LLC Manager. What this means is that a creditor who has obtained a Charging Order only has the right to receive distributions from the entity when and if such distributions are made—even though the entity itself may have substantial income. The Charging Order remedy is often the exclusive remedy available to the creditor and provides substantial Asset Protection for the LLC owner.

8. What about Putting Real Estate in the LLC?

If the primary purpose of the LLC is to hold title to a real estate investment, the members will need to deed or convey the real property involved to the LLC by means of a formal deed that needs to be recorded. All of the rents with respect to the real property should be deposited in the LLC bank account, and all expenses with respect to the property should be paid for out of the LLC bank account. All contracts with respect to the real property and service arrangements should be exclusively in the name of the LLC.

9. What Are Some Examples?

The following are some examples of when and why an LLC might be wisely selected:

a. Jean Simon is a widow, who—in addition to her residence—owns a four-plex in Santa Ana, California. She is concerned about potential liability above and beyond what insurance would cover and has elected to place the four-plex into an LLC of which she is the single member. She treats it as a disregarded entity for tax purposes and all of the tax and accounting are reported on her individual return.

b. Dave Carson, his brother Bill, and their friend Richard, each own a one-third interest in a small shopping center in Long Beach, California. They have created an LLC in which to hold title to the shopping center so as to protect their respective personal assets from any claims with respect to the shopping center. All three of them participate equally in the LLC (which is Member-managed by the three of them) and treat it as a partnership for tax purposes. The LLC files a partnership Return; and Dave, Bill, and Richard each receive a K-1, the information of which they report on their own individual tax returns.

c. Ron Tolberg owns a 25% interest in a 76-unit apartment building that he manages in Anaheim, California. The other 75% is owned by various members of Ron's family and by some friends. Ron has placed the apartment complex into an LLC—which is a Manager-managed LLC since Ron is the one who does all of the management duties and responsibilities. The LLC reports its taxes as a partnership, and Ron and all the other members receive K-1 forms for their shares of profits. Ron also receives a salary or guaranteed payment as Manager, which is paid to him as an expense before there is a division of profits.

   d. The LLC can also be used to operate a retail or other business in a situation where limited liability is desirable, but the flexibility of the LLC is required.

APPENDIX

C

Post-Incorporation Memorandum

Memorandum

TO:

FROM: JEFFREY R. MATSEN

DATE:

RE: POST-INCORPORATION PROCEDURES

The legal formalities of setting up and establishing your corporation have now been completed. Your Articles of Incorporation have been filed in the Office of the California Secretary of State; your By-laws have been adopted; your corporate Minutes have been prepared and properly executed, and the records of the issuance of your shares of stock are completed.

The transition of your business to a corporation may seem to be a little foreign and somewhat complex to you. To facilitate this transition, we suggest that you read this Memorandum and keep it easily accessible for future reference.

1. The Articles of Incorporation are the essential legal document that serves as a charter from the State of California for you to operate as a corporation. They are very broad and general in nature and would only require amendment in the event of a change of name or some sort of a substantial capital reorganization of the corporation.

2. The By-laws of the corporation provide the officers, directors, and shareholders with formal rules of procedures and protocol with respect to the government of the corporation.

3. The Minutes of the corporation memorialize the actions taken by the shareholders and directors with respect to the important transactions of the corporation. Generally speaking, the shareholders should plan on having an annual shareholders meeting which is designated in the By-laws to be held on the _____ of _____ at _____ a.m., (except for the year _____). At this annual meeting, the shareholders will elect the directors of the corporation for the coming year and ratify the actions of the directors for the previous year. Further shareholder action is required only in the event of major structural transactions such as a corporate reorganization or a sale of substantially all of the assets of the corporation.

4. The directors of the corporation are empowered to elect the corporate officers and to approve, ratify, and authorize significant corporate actions. The directors should also meet at least once a year in conjunction with the annual shareholders meeting.

5. We would suggest that you keep notes of these important transactions and that from time to time you contact our office and request our assistance in the preparation of your corporate Minutes. These memorialize the important actions taken by the directors and shareholders of your corporation. In any event, it is extremely important that you maintain the formal integrity of your new corporation and that all major transactions in your business be properly documented in the Minutes of the meetings of your board of directors. The Internal Revenue Service places great emphasis on corporate Minutes; therefore, they should be professionally prepared and documented. In lieu of meetings, the shareholders and directors can ratify and authorize action in the form of unanimous written resolutions.

6. It is the responsibility of the officers and directors of the corporation to make certain that accounting practices and auditing procedures customarily followed by similar businesses are observed in a proper and timely fashion by the corporation. Accordingly, you should follow up on the initial steps we have taken to form your corporation. We have obtained a Federal Employer Identification Number for your corporation, which is _____. If you have employees from whom wages are withheld, you should also file an application for a California employer's identification number. Your accountant can file this application for you. It may be necessary for your corporation to comply with state business licensing requirements or to obtain a relevant city or county license. Please feel free to consult with us should you have any questions with respect to these licenses. It may also be necessary for you to obtain a sales and use tax permit from the State Board of Equalization. As an employer, the corporation should obtain worker's compensation insurance or a certificate of consent to self-insure.

7. Your accountant will assist you in meeting all record-keeping requirements imposed upon your business with respect to financial and tax matters. The fiscal year of your corporation has been determined to be from January 1 to December 31.

8. You have elected Subchapter S treatment for your Corporation (an S Corporation). Generally speaking, an S Corporation is not subject to federal tax on its income at the corporate level. Instead, and unlike a regular C Corporation, income is passed through to the shareholders who, in turn, are taxed directly. Consequently, use of the Subchapter S election enables shareholders to avoid the imposition of double taxation at the corporate and shareholder levels that usually occurs when a C Corporation distributes earnings as a dividend, a liquidating distribution or redemption distribution. **You have also elected to have your Corporation treated as an S Corporation for purposes of California income tax.**

9. If your Corporation is going to do business under a fictitious firm name (i.e., John Doe Enterprises, Inc., dba Pacific Coast Packaging), you will need to file and have published a Fictitious Firm Name Statement in each county where the Corporation does business or owns property. If you file the Fictitious Firm Name Statement, you can utilize the Fictitious Firm Name with respect to all of the procedural steps set forth in Section 10, below. The only exception would be that in setting up your bank accounts you will want to set them up in the official name of the Corporation, but with the caveat that the Corporation does do business under the fictitious firm name. The bank will require a copy of the Fictitious Firm Name Statement, along with a copy of the Articles of Incorporation, the Minutes showing who the Officers and Directors of the Corporation are and, possibly, the Statement by Domestic Stock Corporation.

10. Certain procedural steps should be taken immediately prior to or at the time of your commencing business in the corporate form:

    a. Your letterheads, billing heads, etc., should be modified or changed to reflect the full name of the corporation.

    b. All of your business cards should be similarly changed to reflect the corporate name.

    c. Your bank checking account should reflect your corporation name. A new bank account opened in the name of the corporation on bank signature cards and forms provided by your bank has already been authorized in the Minutes of the first meeting of the board of directors. Call your bank and ask for copies of your new corporate account signature cards and other required authorizations. Send a copy of the bank signature card to us for insertion in the minute book. Anytime you open up new accounts or deal with financial institutions, a copy of the form resolutions you sign should be sent to us for proper filing in the minute book.

    d. Your telephone listing and your listing in all directories should be changed to reflect the corporate name as the opportunity arises.

    e. All leases, contracts and other arrangements you have regarding your present equipment, office premises or furniture, and any other contracts or arrangements that you have previously entered into in connection with your business should be modified, assigned or rewritten in order to reflect the fact that the corporation is now the contracting party to each such lease, contract, or obligation.

    f. The name on your office building, your factory, on the door of your office, on the directory or any other signs you presently exhibit should be changed to reflect your new corporate name.

g. Your insurance should be carefully reviewed to determine if the corporate business is properly insured and that both the corporation and you as an individual are properly protected.

h. You should remember that the corporation is an entity entirely independent and autonomous from the shareholders and officers and directors of the corporation. No personal expenditures or private transactions should be made by the corporation. All loans and other transactions between the corporation and the shareholders should be carefully documented and only entered into after consultation with our firm and your accountants.

i. Within nine months of incorporating, you should notify the Franchise Tax Board of the State of California of the adoption of your fiscal year. By the 15th day of the third month after the close of your first fiscal year, you should file your federal and state income tax returns or obtain an extension.

j. Every year, you are required to file with the Secretary of State a Statement by Domestic Stock Corporation, which our firm will be happy to fill out for you. We have already filed this statement for your first year.

You must pay $800 to the Franchise Tax Board within 3½ months of the date of incorporation for the succeeding fiscal year of the corporation, and thereafter you must pay an $800 franchise tax fee each year. The fee is currently waived for the first year. Please make arrangements with the Franchise Tax Board or your accountant to make this payment in a timely fashion. The initial $800 payment is not related in any way to the tax that will be payable on the income of the first year, and it cannot be used as a credit or offset against the tax that is payable on that income—although in subsequent years, it can be a credit or offset.

11. The State of California carefully regulates the offer and sale of corporate stock, and an offer to sell stock is treated the same as a sale itself. You should always consult with us before you offer to issue or sell any stock of your corporation or before you consider selling substantially all of the assets of the corporation or terminating the corporation. There are extremely significant tax and legal consequences to the foregoing actions, and it is vitally important that you be aware of the ramifications and consequences of these events. The corporation is not dissolved by reason of the death or disqualification of the sole remaining shareholder. Dissolution is accomplished only as provided by the corporate law of the State of California. No pension or profit sharing plan or other compensation arrangement should be terminated or altered without careful review and study by competent legal advisors.

We trust that the foregoing will prove helpful and that the operation of your business as a corporation will be successful and profitable. We are pleased to have been of service to you in the incorporation process and look forward to a lasting and mutually beneficial relationship in the future.

APPENDIX

D

Post-Organization Memorandum (For LLC)

Memorandum

TO:

FROM: JEFFREY R. MATSEN

DATE:

RE: POST-ORGANIZATION PROCEDURES FOR ABC123, LLC, A NEVADA LIMITED LIABILITY COMPANY (LLC)

The legal formalities of setting up and establishing your LLC have now been completed. Your Articles of Organization (LLC-1) have been filed in the Office of the Secretary of State of Nevada, and your Operating Agreement has been drafted and properly executed.

The transition of your business or real estate to an LLC may seem a little foreign and somewhat complex to you. To facilitate this transition, we suggest that you read this Memorandum and keep it easily accessible for future reference.

1. The Articles of Organization (LLC-1) are the essential legal document that serves as a charter from the State of Nevada for you to operate as an LLC. They are very broad and general in nature and would only require amendment in the event of a change of name or some form of management of the LLC.

2. The Operating Agreement sets forth the rights and duties of the Members of the LLC and provides the guidelines for its operation. It deals with capital contributions, allocations and distributions, management, membership notice and voting rights, transfers of membership interests, dissolution and winding up, and other important matters. The LLC can either be managed by the member owners, much like a General Partnership, or it can be structured to be managed by a manager, subject only to the general review and confirmation of the members. In your case, you have chosen to have the LLC be managed by a Manager, who is _____.

3. It is the responsibility of the Manager of the LLC to make certain that accounting practices and auditing procedures customarily followed by similar businesses are observed in a proper and timely fashion. Accordingly, you should follow up on the initial steps we have taken to form your LLC. We have obtained a federal employer identification number for your LLC, which is _____.

4. Your accountant will assist you in meeting all record-keeping requirements imposed upon your business with respect to financial and tax matters. The fiscal year of your LLC has been determined to be from January 1 to December 31.

5. If the primary purpose of your LLC is to hold title to a real estate investment, you will need to deed or convey the real property involved to the LLC by means of a formal deed that needs to be recorded. All of the rents with respect to the real property placed into the LLC should be deposited in the LLC bank account, and all expenses with respect to the property should be paid for out of the LLC bank account. All contracts with respect to the real property and service arrangements should be exclusively in the name of the LLC.

6. If your LLC is going to do business under a fictitious firm name (i.e., XYZ Enterprises, LLC., dba Pacific Coast Packaging), you will need to file and have published a Fictitious Firm Name Statement in each county where the LLC does business or owns property. If you file the Fictitious Firm Name Statement, you can utilize the Fictitious Firm Name with respect to all of the procedural steps set forth in Section 7 below. The only exception would be that in setting up your bank accounts, you will want to set them up in the official name of the LLC, but with the caveat that the LLC does do business under the fictitious firm name. The bank will require a copy of the Fictitious Firm Name Statement, along with a copy of the Articles of Organization (LLC-1) and the Operating Agreement.

7. Certain procedural steps should be taken immediately prior to or at the time of your commencing business in the LLC form:

  a. Your letterheads, billing heads, etc., should be modified or changed to reflect the full name of the LLC.
  b. All of your business cards should be similarly changed to reflect the LLC name.
  c. Your bank checking account should reflect your LLC name.
  d. Your telephone listing and your listing in all directories should be changed to reflect the LLC name as the opportunity arises.
  e. All leases, contracts and other arrangements regarding your present equipment, office premises or furniture, and any other contracts or arrangements that you have previously entered into in connection with your business should be modified, assigned, or rewritten in order to

reflect the fact that the LLC is now the contracting party to each such lease, contract or obligation.

f. The name on your office building, your factory, on the door of your office, on the directory or any other signs you presently exhibit should be changed to reflect your new LLC name.

g. Your insurance should be carefully reviewed to determine if the LLC business is properly insured and that both the LLC and you as an individual are properly protected.

h. You should remember that the LLC is an entity entirely independent and autonomous from the members and the Manager of the LLC. No personal expenditures or private transactions should be made by the LLC. All loans and other transactions between the LLC and the members should be carefully documented and only entered into after consultation with our firm and your accountants.

i. Every year, you are required to file with the Nevada Secretary of State an Annual List of Manager or Managing Members and Resident Agent. We have already filed the Initial List for each LLC for your first year.

j. Your LLC has been registered to do business in the State of California. Therefore, the following information is relevant:

1. LLCs are subject to a Gross Receipts Tax imposed by the California Franchise Tax Board. For LLCs whose revenue is between $250,000 and $499,999, the additional fee is $900. The fee increases to $2,500 for revenues between $500,000 and $999,999, $6,000 for revenues between $1,000,000 and $4,999,999, and $11,790 for revenue of $5,000,000 or more. See California Corporations Code Section 17942(a)(1–3).

2. Every year you are required to file with the Secretary of State a Statement of Information, which our firm will be happy to fill out for you. We have already filed this statement for your first year.

3. You must pay $800 to the Franchise Tax Board on the 15th day of the 4th month after the beginning of your fiscal year. For the first year, it is the 15th day of the 4th month from the date the LLC was organized.

We trust that the foregoing will prove helpful and that the operation of your business or ownership of your real estate as an LLC will be successful and profitable. We are pleased to have been of service to you in the organization process and look forward to a lasting and mutually beneficial relationship in the future.

APPENDIX

Why Use Family Limited Liability Companies?

Estate Planning experts and professionals often refer to Family Limited Partnerships (FLPs) and Family Limited Liability Companies (FLLCs). Most professionals now utilize FLLCs instead of FLPs because FLLCs are less complicated to form, and the Manager of the FLLC is not personally liable (whereas the general partner of a limited partnership is). Because the General Partner is personally liable, another liability-shielded entity like an LLC or a corporation has to be formed to be the General Partner. This is an additional expense, inconvenience and complication that the FLLC avoids. The following explanation helps to understand why the use of FLLCs can be so advantageous.

1. What is an FLLC?

An FLLC can be utilized in your estate plan for making "leveraged" or "discounted" gifts to your children. An FLLC is simply a partnership arrangement between family members. Typically, the FLLC is established by parents or grandparents for purposes of making gifts to junior family members, while allowing the senior family members to maintain full control over the management and investment decisions relating to all of the underlying FLLC property.

2. How Do You Organize and Set Up an FLLC?

To establish an FLLC, the parents would transfer property to the FLLC in exchange for a 100% member interest thereof. Typically, the parents would hold the member interest as Trustees of their Family Trust.

In the beginning, the parents would be the managers of the FLLC with sole control over the FLLC and its property. At some point in time, the parents would begin gifting a portion of their 100% member interests in the FLLC to their children, but continue to retain complete control over the day-to-day investment and management decisions relating to the property. The junior members do not have to have any voice in the management of the FLLC.

3.   What Are the Asset Protection Features of the FLLC?

One of the strongest reasons for creating an FLLC for real estate is that the FLLC protects the real estate owner's personal assets from attack by the creditors of the FLLC. The FLLC itself is liable for its debts and claims against it and the asset that it holds, but the owners of the FLLC are not liable for these claims. For example, if you personally own a rental duplex, and someone is injured at the duplex, if the injury claim is not covered by insurance (either because the insurance amount was insufficient or the claim was excluded from coverage), then the person asserting the claim can not only go against the rental property, but also against all of the owner's other personal and business assets. However, if the duplex is owned by an FLLC, the claim can only be made against the FLLC and the property within the FLLC; the other assets of the owner cannot be attacked. There are also some other Asset Protection feature to FLLCs, but they are beyond the scope of this article.

4.   How Does the FLLC Save Estate Taxes?

The FLLC can also be drafted to provide that the children members will not be allowed to transfer their member interests during their lifetime without the consent of the other members. This restriction on the transfer of the member interests will discount the value of the gifted FLLC interest for gift tax purposes by reducing its marketability (Marketability Discount). Because the children members will not have any voice in the management of the FLLC, the value of the gifted FLLC interest will be discounted to reflect this lack of control (Control Discount). Combined, these two discounts are sometimes referred to as the Minority Discount and typically reduce the value of the transferred interest for gift tax purposes by 20–60%, depending on what type of assets are held by the FLLC. (A greater discount is typically allowed when the assets held by the FLLC are not readily marketable, e.g., closely-held securities, interests in real estate, etc.)

5.   How Do Senior Family Members Retain Control over FLLC Property?

The parents can maintain control over the FLLC property for as long as they like. This plan can be drafted to make the parents the manager with sole management control over the FLLC. The children can have as much or as little control as the parents want them to have.

6.   Does the FLLC Allow Me to Transfer Control to My Children?

The FLLC is an ideal vehicle to transfer control of the family business or other property to your children as quickly or as gradually as you wish. Often, the first step to developing responsibility in children is to provide them with a small share of the family business or family investment property that will attract and develop their interest. The FLLC is flexible enough to allow you to transfer control and responsibility of the business or investment as you see fit.

7. Why and When Should I Start Making Gifts to My Children?

After the FLLC has been established, your FLLC could be used as part of your estate plan to make "discounted" lifetime gifts to your children. Alternatively, the interest in your FLLC could be held until the first of your deaths, after which time the surviving spouse could then begin making gifts of the FLLC interests to your children. This second use of an FLLC has a double benefit; the survivor will receive a full step-up in basis of the underlying FLLC assets for income tax purposes after the first death, and following the survivor's death, the FLLC interest could still be discounted for estate tax purposes.

8. How Can the FLLC Help Me Make Discounted Lifetime Gifts?

If you establish an FLLC and subsequently make lifetime gifts of the FLLC interests to your children, the FLLC interest would entitle your children to all of the economic benefits from their gifted FLLC interest, but without any management authority relating to the FLLC property. Because of the restriction, as discussed above, the FLLC interest has a reduced value. The value of any FLLC interest you give to your children during your lifetime will be removed from your estate for estate tax purposes. Following your death, only the value of any remaining FLLC interest you still own will be includible in your estate for estate tax purposes.

   The restriction on transfer referred to above has an added benefit when the FLLC interests are gifted to your children, since the restriction will provide some protection from a child's judgment creditor (such as a divorced spouse). A child's creditor will not be allowed to reach the underlying FLLC assets to satisfy a judgment, but rather will only be entitled to the child's economic interest in the FLLC—i.e., the right to FLLC distributions, if any.

9. How Does the Reduced Value Help with Annual Giving?

The Minority Discount of the value of the FLLC interests allows you to effectively make larger annual tax free gifts. For example: If for gift tax purposes, a 40% discount is allowed for the FLLC interest (due to the Minority Discount), you could transfer FLLC interests representing up to $21,667 in "underlying" FLLC assets without exceeding your annual gift tax exclusion of $13,000 per donee ($21,667 × 60% = $13,000). Under current law, your annual gift tax exclusion allows you to transfer up to $13,000 per year to each individual without such transfer being subject to gift tax; together, you and your spouse can transfer up to $26,000 per year (in the above example, your combined annual gift tax exclusions would allow for a transfer of $43,334 in "pre-discount" FLLC interests). As can be seen by this example, the discount associated with your gifted FLLC interests will allow you to transfer a greater amount of "underlying" FLLC assets without exceeding the amount of your annual exclusions from gift tax.

Continuing this example, if you wish to use your unified credit to shelter the gift tax on FLLC interests in excess of your annual exclusion amount, $8,333,333 in FLLC interests could be transferred without exceeding the $5,000,000 amount sheltered from tax by your unified credit ($8,333,333 × 60% = $5,000,000). Under current law, your unified credit will shelter the first $5,000,000 of transferred assets (whether during your lifetime) from gift tax. Using the above example of a 40% discount in the value of the FLLC interests, if both you and your spouse wish to use your unified credits to transfer FLLC interests to your children, up to $16,666,667 in underlying FLLC assets could be transferred without paying any gift tax ($16,666,667 × 60% = $10,000,000).

It should be noted that the estate and gift tax credit is currently scheduled to be reduced to $1 million starting January 1, 2013, unless Congress acts sooner to change or keep the current law. No one knows what will happen, but we will publicize any changes on our Website at www.wealthstrategiescounsel.com.

F

Asset Protection and Marital Planning

Community Property and the Division of Community Property between Spouses

California is a community property state, and under California law:

1. The Community property is generally property acquired during the marriage and any separate property that may have been transmuted into community property or commingled with marital property.

2. All post marital accumulations are community property. See California Family Code Section 760.

3. Community property generally is liable for the debts incurred by either spouse. See Family Code Section 910. In other words, the community estate is liable for a debt incurred by either spouse before or during marriage irrespective of which spouse has the management and control of the community estate and regardless of whether one or both spouses are parties to the debt or to a judgment for the debt.

4. In this regard, it should be noted that it is the community estate and not the non-debtor spouse that incurs the liability. There are no "community debts," only "debts for which community property is liable." See *Lezine v. Security Pacific Financial Services, Inc. 58 Cal Rptr. 2d 76 (1996).*

5. On the other hand, the spouse's separate property is liable only for that spouse's debts. See Family Code Section 913.

Transmutation

Under California law, a married couple can transmute community property into separate property. See Family Code Section 850. The agreement of spouses to separate and divide their community property whether by formal written contract or informal transmutation between themselves will be enforced. See *Kennedy v. Taylor 201 Cal. Rptr. 779, 781 (4th Dist. Ct, App. 1984)*. Under *The Kennedy Case*, informal transmutation will be binding on third parties, including creditors. Any separate property that has been transmuted from community property cannot be reached by creditors. The intended outcome under California law is to protect a separate and non-contracting spouse from the debtor spouse's obligation. See *Kennedy, Supra at 201 Cal. Rptr. at 780.* Parenthetically, it should be noted if the debtor spouse receives primarily exempt and illiquid assets, it may be that the creditor's recovery has been diminished by more than 50%.

Transmutation and the Fraudulent Transfer Laws

Transmutation is subject to the fraudulent transfer laws. See Family Code Section 851. However, in a transmutation process where each spouse receives equivalent amounts as separate property, each spouse will be treated as having given fair value, thereby avoiding the application of the fraudulent transfer laws. See *Britt v. Damson 334 F. 2nd: 896, 903 (9th Cir. 1964), cert. den., 379 US 966 (1965).* See also *In re Chappel, 243F. Supp. 417 (S.D. Cal 1965).*

However, community property transferred to the non-debtor spouse as part of the distribution of community assets upon dissolution of marriage may still be liable for the debts of the debtor spouse. See Family Code Section 916. The following summary of cases is relevant with respect to the application of Section 916:

a. In the case of *In re Marriage of Braendle*, 54 Cal. Rptr 2d. 397 (1996), the Court found that "once the marriage was dissolved and division of community property had occurred, [. . .] the provisions of Section 916 of the Family Code control." Therefore, the separate property of the non-debtor spouse allocated to him or her by the marital settlement agreement cannot be attached by the creditor of the debtor spouse.

b. In *The Lezine Case* previously cited, the Court, in commenting on the predecessor to Family Code Section 916, observed: "Under this provision, following the division of property, the community property awarded to one spouse is no longer liable for marital debts that are assigned to the other spouse, with the exception that the award of community real property to one spouse that is subject to a lien remains liable for satisfaction of the lien, i.e., the lien remains enforceable to satisfy the underlying debt."

c. In *Gagan v. Gouyd, 73 Cal. App. 4th 835 (4th Dist. Ct. App. 1999)*, the Court held "that to engraft the fraudulent transfer remedies onto a valid and approved marital settlement agreement would result in needlessly complicating the already emotionally laden dissolution process." The Court further cited *California Practice Guide: Family Law* (the Rutter Group, 1999), Paragraph 8:778 at Page 8–191: "unless the non debtor

[sic] spouse was assigned the debt by the property division judgment, he or she is not personally liable thereafter for the other spouse's debts incurred before or during marriage. The non debtor [sic] spouse's separate property and his or her share of the community estate awarded by the dissolution judgment may be reached by creditors only if payment of the debt was assigned to the non debtor [sic] spouse in the property division."

  d. After *The Gagan Case*, the 6th *District (Santa Clara County)* issued its decision in *Mejia v. Reed, 97 Cal. App. 4th 277; 118 Cal Rptr. 2nd 415 (6th Dist. Ct. App. 2002)*. In Mejia, the Court held that marital property settlements and judgments are subject to the fraudulent transfer laws and specifically rejected the holding in Gagan. However, it appears that the bankruptcy court will accord substantial weight to a determination by the state court in a marriage dissolution proceeding even though made as a non-contested ruling approving the party settlement. (See *Britt v. Damson* and In *Re Chappel* cited above.)

  e. Subsequently, the defendant in *Mejia v. Reed* sought review of the judgment from the Court of Appeal, 6th District (Santa Clara County) decision. In *Mejia v. Reed, 3 Cal. Rptr. 3d. 390 (2003)*, the Supreme Court of California held that the Uniform Fraudulent Transfer Act (UFTA) applied to property transfers under marital settlement agreements. The court determined, however, that there was no triable issue of fact as to constructive fraud. The discounted value of future child support, because it was generally paid from future income rather than current assets, was not to be considered as a debt in determining solvency under Cal. Civ. Code § 3439.05. Thus, the Defendant was not rendered insolvent by the transfer. Actual fraud, however, was a triable issue.

Conclusion

In view of the foregoing, a transmutation or marital settlement agreement is subject to avoidance as a fraudulent conveyance. However, see *State Board of Equalization vs. Woo 98 Cal Rptr. 2d 206 (2000), (Rehrg denied, August 7, 2002)*, wherein the California Court of Appeals held that a wife's attempt to transmute her future earnings into separate property in order to avoid her husband's existing tax debt constituted a fraudulent transfer in violation of Family Code Section 851.

One of the problems of transmuting community property into separate property is the loss of the step-up in basis that would otherwise occur upon the death of the transferor spouse. If property is classified as community property under state law, upon the death of the first spouse, the entire property (even the community property one-half ownership interest of the surviving spouse) receives the step-up in basis for income tax purposes. Accordingly, the surviving spouse can thereafter sell such property and there will be little, if any, gain on the sale as a result of the step-up in basis. However, if community property is transmuted into separate property either by gift or by means of the marital settlement agreement, when the transferor spouse predeceases the transferee spouse, there will be no step-up in basis at that time with respect to the property transferred.

G

Bullet-Proofing Your Corporation

Many small business owners are well aware of the importance and benefits of incorporation. If properly formed and operated, a corporation shields its shareholders from personal liability.

While many small business owners seek legal counsel to assist them with formation of their corporation, they may not understand the benefits of having continuing legal counsel to assist with the operation of their corporation—specifically the importance of maintaining corporate formalities. Failure to draft and maintain documents related to the operation of your corporation may subject the corporation to fines from state agencies, civil liability, and, at worst, the ability of courts to disregard the corporate form and make shareholders personally liable for debts of the corporation.

Though you may believe that your business is a small, private company that does not need to follow the rules for large, public companies, the law does not make exceptions—only subtle distinctions that your attorney can explain to you.

What Is Required?

Upon the formation of your corporation, you must submit Articles of Incorporation to the Secretary of State in your domicile. The Articles of Incorporation must have specific clauses by law. If you have a closely held corporation, you must include additional clauses specified by law. No corporation may issue shares until the Articles are approved by the Commissioner of Corporations. Your corporation must also draft and adopt bylaws, laying out the rules adopted by the corporation for its internal governance.

Annually, a corporation must file a Statement of Information with the Secretary of the State to remain in good standing.

Prior to issuing any stock, even a so-called "private" company may be required to either register the stock with the relevant state corporate agency or request an exemption. Your attorney can assist you with filing for the proper exemption to ensure your stock is properly authorized and issued, even if you—or you and your spouse—are the only shareholders. Your attorney may even be able to properly exempt shares previously issued improperly.

Corporations must also hold shareholder meetings annually and must keep Minutes of such meetings. Corporate decisions must be documented and ratified, either by director meetings or by resolutions by directors passed by unanimous written consent. Proper notice must be given for all meetings, as specified in the bylaws. Your attorney can assist you in ensuring you maintain the proper Minutes and resolutions for all corporate decisions.

A corporation must maintain proper accounting records and shareholder records. Even a change in the name of one of the shareholders, or (for example) a transfer of title from your personal name to the name of your Revocable Living Trust, must be properly documented in the corporate records book.

Failure to Comply Can Harm You

Failure to comply with the above formalities can subject you to monetary fines, personal liability, or even loss of control over your business.

If you do not annually file the Statement of Information with the state, the Franchise Tax Board may impose fines on your corporation. Failure to file for two consecutive years could lead the Secretary of State to suspend your corporate rights, powers, and privileges.

Failure to properly separate the affairs of your corporation and personal affairs may also allow a court to determine that the shareholders of a corporation are personally liable for corporate debts, which would eliminate one of the major benefits of the corporate form. A court may take into account a number of factors before making a determination, among them commingling corporate and personal funds, treatment of corporate assets as personal assets, failure to obtain authority to issue stock or improperly issued stock, failure to maintain Minutes or adequate corporate records, and disregard of legal formalities among related entities.

Keeping good records and tight control over the corporation is especially important if you have business partners. Your business partner may take actions on behalf of the corporation that you may not be aware of if you do not maintain strict control over corporate activities by complying with the above rules. The actions taken by partners may lead to corporate or even personal liability. Furthermore, disputes amongst business partners can quickly escalate into very expensive litigation. Many of these disputes arise in corporations where actions taken by directors and/or officers are not properly documented, and one party may take advantage of the lax oversight of corporate affairs. Maintaining complete corporate records and retaining knowledgeable corporate counsel can save you substantial litigation expenses and fines, and provide invaluable stress relief.

APPENDIX

H

For Whom the Bell Toll

Over the last few decades, expanding theories of liability and the proliferation of litigation has given increased emphasis for Asset Protection Planning to the extent that it is now a well-recognized area of practice. We live in a victim-oriented society where aggressive plaintiff lawyers are always trying to find the "deep pocket." There is increased media and social awareness of large plaintiffs' judgments and a high level of notoriety for malpractice and other errors-and-omissions types of lawsuits. Obviously, there are individuals who are more at risk, such as professionals like physicians, dentists, lawyers, CPAs, architects, engineers, etc. Business owners and any individuals dealing with investors also face tremendous liability exposure. A seller of a business has to worry about a purchaser with buyer's remorse who can sue for fraud, misrepresentation, and failure to disclose. Many business owners and real estate investors have to sign personal guarantees in order to carry on their business activities and purchase their real estate assets. Anyone who owns a boat, an airplane or an extreme vehicle faces tremendous liability potential. Individuals with high risk businesses such as waste refuge or recycling are concerned about environmental claims liability.

All of these types of individuals generate terrific liability exposure. But what about the non-professional or non-business owner—the average individual who is not engaging in a liability-related activity? Does the average person really need Asset Protection Planning?

Recently, I met with a retired couple who have a very nice home here in Southern California which is completely paid off, a reasonable pension and IRA assets, and a little over $250,000 in cash and marketable securities. They had a California Revocable Living Trust, but really didn't think there was any reason for them to worry about Asset Protection Planning. However, a few weeks before our meeting, the wife had been involved in a major automobile accident, as a result of which, one of the passengers in the other car became permanently paralyzed. The couple was now facing a lawsuit of several million dollars. Their insurance coverage was limited to $500,000. Their entire savings and their beautiful home are now at risk. Who would have thought?

A few weeks ago, I met with another couple who own a small family business that is reasonably profitable and provides both of them with a good income. The business is involved in the distribution of non-high-risk products, but my clients were still concerned about potential liability from various sources dealing with their business. They were also concerned, however, about personal liability with respect to normal, everyday activities like owning and operating automobiles, utilizing their power speed boat and other activities that they engage in at their vacation home on a recreational lake. As we discussed their exposure situation, they related to me that they had often talked about their potential risks, and they were very excited that I was able to address their concerns and structure a plan that would afford them much more protection than they would otherwise have had.

The point is, of course, that everyone needs to think about Asset Protection Planning. Most people need to review their liability and umbrella insurance coverage. Real estate should be transferred to LLCs. Consideration should be given to transferring personal residences to Domestic Asset Protection Trusts. The fact is, that most individuals who have assets at a value approaching one million dollars or more need to carefully consider an Asset Protection structure. The structure does not need to be that complicated for smaller estates, but Asset Protection must be addressed and reviewed by almost everyone.

APPENDIX

I

How to Avoid Veil-Piercing

One of the principal legal benefits for business owners and real estate investors in using LLCs to conduct their businesses and hold their real estate is the limited liability shield provided by LLC statutes to LLC members and managers. This shield protects the personal assets of these members and managers (e.g., their homes and savings) from being at risk for debts of the LLC and the business assets and real estate the LLC owns.

However, in certain circumstances, the courts may "pierce the veil" of an LLC—that is, they may disregard this shield and may hold members and/or Managers personally liability for claims against the LLC.

Thus, it is critically important for LLC managers ("manager" refers both to the managers of the Manager-managed LLCs and to the members of Member-managed LLCs) to take all reasonable measures to prevent LLC veil-piercing. The principal such measures are outlined below:

1. LLC Managers Should Not Use the LLC to Commit Fraud or Other Serious Misconduct

The courts are unlikely to pierce an LLC's veil unless the members or Manager of the LLC use it to commit fraud or other serious misconduct and then seek to rely on their limited liability shield to avoid personal liability for this misconduct. Thus, to avoid veil-piercing (and, obviously, for many other strong legal and ethical reasons), LLC members and managers should avoid all such misconduct.

2. LLC Managers Should Expressly Refer to Their LLC as an LLC

In general, whenever LLC managers mention their LLC to third parties verbally or in writing, they should expressly refer to it as an LLC. This practice is an effective means of telling third parties that they are dealing with the LLC, not with the LLC's members and managers in their individual capacities, and that, accordingly, they may look only to the LLC and not to the members or managers for satisfaction of claims against the LLC.

Thus, for example, members and managers should generally ensure that the initials "LLC" or the like appear after the names of the LLC in its stationery and invoices, on the business cards of its managers and employees, and on other printed material prepared by the LLC, and communicated to third parties. In addition, LLC members and managers should generally refer to their company in conversations with clients, suppliers, and others as "my LLC" rather than merely as "my company" or the like.

However, LLC managers should feel free to depart from the above practices when marketing considerations or other common sense concerns dictate. For example, the initials "LLC" may sometimes appear odd and out-of-place on a street sign identifying a store that does business as an LLC, or in a newspaper advertisement of the store.

3. LLC Managers Should Maintain Separate Books and Bank Accounts for Themselves in Their Individual Capacities and for the LLC

A basic rationale for the limited liability shield that LLCs afford to their members and managers is the legal separateness of LLCs vis-à-vis their members and managers. Thus, to protect the shield, members and managers should take every reasonable step to implement and document this separateness. For example:

- They should keep separate books and bank accounts for, on the one hand, the personal affairs of members and managers, and on the other, the business and affairs of the LLC.
- They should not write checks from the LLC's account for personal use, nor should they deposit money in that account, without making and maintaining written records of these transactions that reflect arm's-length terms.

4. LLC Managers Should Ensure that at the Time of Its Formation and Thereafter, the LLC Is Adequately Capitalized

Some courts may question the propriety of the conduct of an LLC and may pierce its veil if the LLC lacks adequate capitalization—that is, if its aggregate equity contributions, business assets, cash flow, insurance, and other financial resources are inadequate to pay its debts when due. Thus, LLC managers should ensure that their LLCs are adequately capitalized.

5. In Acting on Behalf of Their LLC, LLC Managers Should Avoid Any Action that May Imply to Third Parties that They Are Acting on Their Own Behalf

In acting on behalf of the LLC, managers should avoid any action that may imply to third parties that they are acting on their own behalf, and where appropriate, they should state explicitly that they are acting on behalf of the LLC. For example, LLC managers should sign LLC contracts and letters more or less as follows:

XYZ, LLC

By _____, Manager

6. LLC Managers Should Ensure Their LLCs Follow All Applicable Formalities Imposed by the Relevant LLC Act

Unlike corporate legislation, LLC legislation typically imposes few, if any, statutory formalities on LLCs. For example, LLC legislation generally does not require LLCs to hold annual meeting of members, and no LLC status requires LLCs to issue certificates of membership to their members.

However, to the extent that the LLC legislation under which an LLC is formed does impose formalities, members and managers should make sure that they comply with them and that they document this compliance.

For example, some LLC status contains provisions requiring the LLC to maintain specified types of records (e.g., tax returns and member lists) at a specified LLC office. Members and managers of LLCs formed under such status should ensure compliance with these provisions.

7. Conclusion

It is important that the foregoing steps be evaluated from time to time in order to ensure that the LLC veil cannot be pierced. In this regard, it is a good idea to review these issues with your attorney on an annual basis.

APPENDIX

J

The Nevada Asset Protection Trust

In most cases, when the individual who creates and transfers assets to a Trust (the maker, Trustor or Settlor of the Trust) is also a beneficiary of that Trust, the Trust provisions will not protect the Settlor/beneficiary's creditors from reaching the assets of the Trust. On the other hand—as we have discussed with Offshore Asset Protection—the law of many foreign jurisdictions provides that when a Settlor transfers assets to an Offshore Asset Protection Trust, that Trust can protect the assets of the Trust even though the Trustor is a beneficiary of the Trust.

In the late 1990s, several states began to reverse the general rule concerning Self-Settled Spend Thrift Trusts and statutorily modified their laws accordingly. This litigation has made these types of Trusts similar to Offshore Asset Protection Trusts. Delaware, Alaska and Nevada are among the 13 states that have adopted such legislation. The Nevada legislation was enacted in 1999 and allows the Trustor to protect the principal of the Trust from Outside creditors even though the Trustor is a beneficiary of the Trust.

This legislation is extremely important and critical to Asset Protect Planning. For many people, the typical Revocable Living Trust they have set up in California or elsewhere provides zero protection against the creditors of the Settlors of the Trust, whether they have a claim arising prior to the establishment of the Trust or after.

Under the relevant provisions of the Nevada law, at least one Trustee must be a Nevada resident. Wealth Strategies Counsel recommends that a Trust company organized under the laws of Nevada be the Trustee of the Nevada Asset Protection Trust. The major advantage of the Nevada laws is the shorter period of time required for protection between the date an asset is transferred to the Trust and the date the protection begins from the creditors of the Trustor. The Nevada statute of limitation in this is only two years, whereas the other principal states have much longer statutes of limitations.

Again, it should be emphasized that only a minority of states permit Self-Settled Asset Protection Trusts. The benefits of using the Nevada Asset Protection Trust are obvious not only from the standpoint of high-net-worth individuals who want to protect their large property holdings, but also for many younger people who are in the process of building their estates and who face high liability exposure—such as doctors, lawyers, and other types of business owners and executives.

One of the best ways to utilize the Nevada Asset Protection Trust is to create a modular structure combining the Nevada Asset Protection Trust with a limited liability company (LLC). Basically, the member interest of the owner of the LLC is transferred to the Nevada Asset Protection Trust, which holds the interest, more or less, as a custodian. For example, a husband or wife can be the Settlor of the Nevada Asset Protection Trust. The LLCs can then be set up to hold real property and other assets, and the member interests of the LLCs can be transferred to the Nevada Asset Protection Trust. It is recommended that a third party own at least 5% of the LLC because the efficacy of the Charging Order remedy limitation of creditors of the LLC is greatly reduced and even eliminated when the LLC is a single-member LLC.

A diagram of the structure is set forth in Figure J.1.

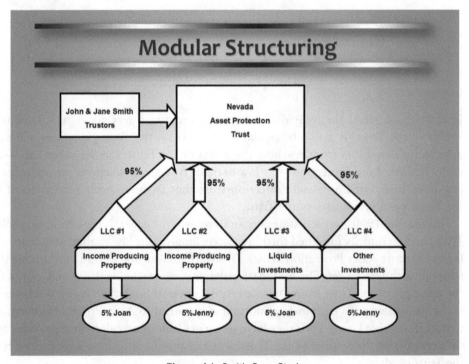

Figure J.1 Smith Case Study

For greater understanding of the Charging Order and LLC, please see Chapter 8.

K

Putting Personal Residences into an FLP or FLCC: A No-No

The question of whether or not a personal family residence should be placed into a Family Limited Partnership (FLP) or Family Limited Liability Company (FLLC) is a frequent topic for discussion. The impetus for such a decision is based on the theory that the FLP or FLLC affords the owner a degree of Asset Protection against personal liability—because a creditor is allegedly limited to a Charging Order Remedy when trying to get at the assets inside the FLP or FLLC. A Charging Order limits the creditor to a distribution right rather than granting it the ability to seize the assets itself within the FLP or FLLC. Whether or not the Charging Order Remedy really effectively precludes a creditor from getting to the assets of the FLP or FLLC is a question I have addressed in other sections of this book. In any case, a creditor does normally have a more difficult time accessing assets that are inside an FLP or an FLLC than if they are held in the owner's individual name.

However, it would not appear that placing a personal residence into an FLP or FLLC will really work. In the first place, a Limited Partnership or Limited Liability Company is supposed to have legitimate business purposes and to be established for a profit. If you place a personal residence into the FLP or FLLC, it would, therefore, appear that you would have to pay rent to the FLP or FLLC in order to make any business sense of the transaction. In fact, placing the residence into the FLP or FLLC could engender several adverse tax consequences, i.e., the loss of the capital gain credit on the sale and the state real property tax exemption.

But, perhaps, the homeowner is willing to tolerate the adverse tax consequences in exchange for the purported Asset Protection benefits. The problem, however, is that it is likely that the courts are going to find (because of the lack of business purposes) that the FLP or FLLC is really a sham. For example, the following language *The Turner Case* (In *re Turner 335 B.R. 140 Bkrpt. N.D. CA. 2005*) very pointedly highlights the problem:

> Asset protection is not illegal and is honored by the law if done for a legitimate purpose. For example, an individual may do business through a corporation or limited liability company and will not be held personally liable for the debts of the entity. The assets of the corporation or a limited liability company will not be considered the assets of the individual interest holder. However, an entity or series of entities may not be created with no business purpose and personal assets transferred to them with no relationship to any business purposes, simply as a means of shielding them from creditors. Under such circumstances, the law views the entity as the alter ego of the individual debtor and will disregard it to prevent injustice.

Therefore, placing a personal residence into an FLP or FLLC is definitely a No-No in most instances.

Are there other Asset Protection Planning techniques available for a personal residence? Definitely.

- First of all, equity stripping should be considered.
- Obtaining a second-trust-deed line of credit is an excellent planning step.
- Transferring the residence to a Domestic Asset Protection Trust is also a very viable alternative.
- Sometimes a transfer to a Qualified Personal Residence Trust (QPRT) or a Non-Qualified Personal Residence Trust may be effective.

In any event, any strategy should be thoroughly discussed with and analyzed by competent legal counsel.

Index

A

Actual intent, 14, 36
Anderson Case, The, 62
Anti-duress, 59
Asset protection, *Throughout*
Attorney rating services
  "AVVO", 78
  Martindale Hubble, 78

B

Badges of fraud, 14
Bankruptcy
  bankruptcy courts, 16
  considerations, 16–17
Beneficiaries, 50, 68
Bonds, 9, 61, 74
Business entity, 20, 27–28, 85–86, 87
Business Planning, 77
Business succession, 32

C

C Corp, 26–27, 93
Certified Public Accountant (CPA), 4, 17, 77, 83, 109
Charging Order
  definition, 42
  history, 42–44
Charitable Lead Trusts, 67
Charitable Remainder Trusts, 67

Claims, *Throughout*
Concealment of asset, 14
Contempt. *See Offshore Trusts, Contempt*
Cook Islands, 60–61
Cook Islands International Trust Act, 61
Corporation, *Throughout*
  C Corporation. *See C Corp*
  double tax, 27, 93
  S Corporation, Subsection S Corporation, Sub S
    Corporation. *See S Corp*
Credit Shelter, 60
Creditors, *Throughout*
Criminal Statutes, 17

D

Deep-Pocket Theory, 8, 75
Dentists
  insurance, 74
  special planning, 72, 74
Discovery Phase, 10
Doctors. *See Physicians*
Domestic Asset Protection Trusts (DAPTs), 5, 50–55
Durable Power of Attorney, 30

E

Employment Retirement Income Security Act (ERISA), 37
Equipment, 39, 73, 82, 93
Equity stripping, 46, 118

Estate Planning, *Throughout*
Estate taxes, 22, 37, 65, 68–69
Exemptions, 36–37
  annuities, 21, 36
  homestead. *See Homestead Exemption*
  insurance, 21, 36
  retirement plans, 21, 37
Exit strategy planning, 27, 32

F
Family Limited Liability Company (FLLC), 66–67,
  99–102, 117–118
Family Limited Partnerships (FLP), 66–67, 99,
  117–118
Federal Employer Identification Number (FEIN), 46
Foreign Asset Protection trusts (FAPT), 49, 58–59, 61–63
Forum shopping, 44
Foundational documents, 29–33
Fraud, 9, 14, 17, 111
Fraudulent conveyance, 11, 15
Fraudulent transfer law, 13–16, 104–105

G
General Partnership, 25
Gifting, 30
Gifts, 60, 66–67, 101
Grantor Retained Annuity Trusts (GRATs), 6, 67–68
Grantor Trusts, 58, 60

H
Health Insurance Portability and Accountability Act
  (HIPAA), 31
Healthcare Directives, 31
Homestead exemption, 21, 36

I
Independent contractor, 9, 72–73
Inheritance, 55, 69
Inside Creditors, 3, 39
Inside Debt, 3, 23, 24, 39–40
Installment sales, 14
Insurance, *Throughout*
  errors and omissions type, need for, 74
  liability insurance, 2–3, 37
  need for, 37
  scope of, 2–3, 4, 5
Intentionally Defective Grantor Trusts, 6
Intentionally Defective Irrevocable Trust (IDITs), 68–69
Investment assets, 21, 39
IRAs, 2, 37
Irrevocable Life Insurance Trusts (ILIT), 6, 65–66, 67

J
Joint ownership of property, 37–38
Judge vs. jury trials, 10

L
Ladder of Success, 19–22
Lawrence Case, The, 62–63
Liability protected entities, 5, 21, 40, 41
Limited Liability Companies (LLCs), *Throughout*
  Family LLCs (FLLCs). *See Family LLCs*
  Manager-managed LLCs, 26, 87–88
  Member-managed LLCs, 26, 87–88
  minority members of the LLC, 47
  multi-member LLCs, 39, 47, 88
  Series LLCs. *See Series LLCs*
  single-member LLCs, 39, 46–47, 52
Limited Partnerships (LPs), 2, 25–26, 66–67
Living Trusts, 31–33, 38, 49, 115

M
Malpractice, 9, 10, 74
Marital Planning, 5, 21, 38, 103–105
Matsen Spectrum of Fraudulent Conveyance
  Applicability, 15
Medical Power of Attorney, 31
Medical practice, *Throughout;. See also Physicians*
  equipment, 73
  independent contractor. *See* Independent contractor
  non-practice assets, 74, 75
  professional relationship agreement. *See* Professional
    relationship agreement
  surgical center, 73
Medical Records Release Form, 31
Minority Discount, 66–67, 100, 101
Modular planning, 21, 63–64
Money laundering, 17
  Money Laundering Control Act, 17
Mortensen Case, The, 17, 51
Multiple liability protected entities, 41

N
Net worth, 7, 9, 19, 83, 85
Nondisclosure, 9

O
Offshore jurisdiction, 59, 60–61
Offshore Trusts
  issues of contempt, 61–63
  maintenance, 58–59
  selecting jurisdiction, 59–60
  setting up, 58–59
  tax considerations, 60
Operating Agreement, 46, 88, 95–96
Outside Creditors, 4
Outside Debt, 4, 41–42

P
Patriot Act, 17
Perjury, 10, 11

Personal Liability, *Throughout*
Physicians
  insurance, 14
  special planning
Plaintiff lawyers, 8, 74, 109
Pour-Over Will, 30, 80
Powers of Attorney, 30, 31
  Durable Power of Attorney. *See* Durable Power
    of Attorney
  Medical Power of Attorney. *See* Medical Power
    of Attorney
Private annuities, 14
Private Retirement Plan, 75
Probate, 31, 32, 49
Professional Relationship Agreements, 73

Q
Qualified Personal Residence Trusts (QPRT),
  6, 46, 68, 118

R
Racketeer Influenced and Corrupt Organizations Act
  (RICO), 17
Real estate assets, 40–41
  insurance, 40
Real estate investors, 3, 109, 111
Rental property, 39
Revocable Living Trusts (RLT), 21
Right attorney, selection of, 77–79

S
S Corporation, 24, 26, 27, 40, 92, 93
Self-Settled Trusts, 16, 21, 49
Series LLCs, 44–45, 46
Sexual harassment claims, 24

Shield of liability, 1–3
Sole Proprietorship, 23, 24–25
State Bar Association, 78
Statute of Elizabeth, 13
Surgical Centers, 72, 73

T
Talent Amendment, 16, 36
Taxes, *Throughout, esp*
Traditional sales, 14
Trust Protectors, 55
Trusts, *Throughout*
  characteristics, *throughout*
  placing assets in, *throughout*
  settlor/trustor/trustors, 31, 32
  structure, *throughout*
  trustee/trustees, 16, 59, 61, 99

U
Uniform Fraudulent Conveyance Act (UFCA),
  13, 105
Uniform Fraudulent Transfers Act (UFTA), 13
Uniform Limited Partnership Act, 42
Uniform Partnership Act, 42

V
Victim-oriented society, 7–8

W
Wealth Strategies Counsel, 19, 115
Wills
  executor, 5, 30
  features of, 30
  pour-over will. *See* Pour-over will
  structure, 32

About the Author

Jeffrey R. Matsen is the founder and managing partner of Matsen Voorhees Mintz LLP. His practice encompasses business formations and transactional matters, Estate Planning, Asset Protection, Probate, tax, and real estate. He has been designated as one of the nation's Top 100 Attorneys by *Worth Magazine* and one of Southern California's Super Lawyers by *Los Angeles Magazine*. He has the highest rating ("AV") by Martindale Hubbell and also ("10 Superb") by AVVO. He has been an adjunct professor at Western State University College of Law, Golden Gate University and Chapman University School of Law. He has also given lectures to various professional groups on areas related to his practice, including limited liability companies, business entity formation and selection, Asset Protection techniques, and other relevant topics. He is a member of the American Bar Association (Real Property and Trust Section), WealthCounsel, and the Society of Trust and Estate Practitioners ("STEP"). He is also a faculty member and fellow of the Center for International Legal Studies in Salzburg, Austria. He graduated cum laude from Brigham Young University, earning a BA degree, and graduated with honours from the University of California at Los Angeles, earning a JD degree.